Rosary Consecration

*Total Consecration to Jesus through Mary
and Her Most Holy Rosary*

TJ Burdick

En Route Books and Media, LLC
Saint Louis, MO

⊕*ENROUTE*
Make the time

En Route Books and Media, LLC
5705 Rhodes Avenue
St. Louis, MO 63109

Cover credit: TJ Burdick

ISBN-13: 978-1-956715-94-1
Library of Congress Control Number: 2019946019

Acknowledgments

I want to first thank Mr. Robert Croft, OP, who supplied me with the foundational knowledge on the four Marian dogma sections of this book. Your love for Our Lady is evident and worthy of imitation. May your contributions to this book richly provide for the salvation of many souls.

I also want to thank Dr. Sebastian Mahfood, OP, for helping this book reach the height of publication. Your devotion to the Blessed Virgin is remarkably commendable. May she continue to bless and guide your tireless efforts to advance God's kingdom.

Finally, thank you to the members of the Dominican Order whose steadfast loyalty to Our Lady has been demonstrated throughout the centuries in the recitation of the Rosary. May these chords and beads wrap you in her love and loosen your tongues to preach truth in a world that needs it so much.

Our Lady of the Rosary, pray for us.

Table of Contents

The Three-Day Purge

Introduction

What if you knew what God's will was for your life right now? What if you had the ability to destroy vice, decrease sin, and cause good works and virtue to flourish? What if you could have the light of God and the plenitude of his graces every single day of your life, leading to true peace in your soul?

That's exactly what you'll pursue through this book. St. Paul told us that we can "attain full knowledge of God's will through perfect wisdom and spiritual insight. Then you will lead a life worthy of the Lord and pleasing to him in every way" (Colossians 1:9b-10).

How do we gain this spiritual insight? Who can we ask to teach us how to submit to God's will in the most perfect way? The answer, of course, is Jesus, the God-man in Whom we have our beginning and end. In-between the Alpha and Omega, our souls drift in the sea of life submitting to the currents of the times and pulling us adrift into spiritual confusion. There is, however, a lifeline that connects us with our Creator. She is at the same time the compass by which we sail toward perfection and the perfect creation formed by Perfection Himself — she is Our Lady, and through her we are adopted into the Holy Family in which we call Jesus our true brother.

This book prepares you for total consecration to Jesus through Mary. It is the most practical, insightful, and accessible way toward becoming a closer disciple of Christ and attaining "full knowledge of God's will through perfect wisdom and spiritual insight." After all, it was Jesus who first submitted His being to Mary and her maternal care for his first thirty years on this earth.

To make it so, we combined the timeless Marian prayer of the Rosary and intertwined its mysteries with St. Pope John Paul II's Apostolic Letter, *Rosarium Virginis Mariae*, and the four Marian Dogmas of her Immaculate Conception, Divine Motherhood, Perpetual Virginity, and her Assumption into Heaven.

While it may sound like a lot of information to take in, we've placed all of the content for each day into a short, 5-minute reflection that will not only prepare you for total consecration but will also invigorate your spirit and advance your intellect. In short, this book is the most comprehensive and the least time-consuming way to prepare yourself for total consecration to Jesus through Mary.

Join thousands of others as we grow closer to Christ through Our Lady's Rosary and the meditation of our Total Consecration to her most perfect graces, none greater than the transformation of our souls to a more perfect union with Christ "in whom we live and move and have our being" (Acts 17:28).

Why Total Consecration through the Rosary?

To consecrate oneself completely to Jesus through Mary is to attain the highest degree of dedication to them. When we make our consecration, we give all that we are — our joys our pains, our triumphs and our defeats, our virtue and our vice. While our Lord is the only one who can rightfully separate the wheat from the chafe of our souls, it is our Lady who nourishes the seed of faith within us. It is only when we will to achieve the highest form of our perfection that we are capable of dying completely to ourselves so that Christ can live within us (Gal. 2:20). Only Mary can take our broken souls and repair them, polish them, and present them to the King who will look on us and say, "This is my son, with whom I am well pleased." It is in total consecration that we submit to God's will entirely and thus put on Christ in every aspect of our lives.

Countless Saints have found their source of holiness in making themselves the servant of Mary in this way. St. Alphonsus Liguori, St. Maximilian

Kolbe, and many others found their spiritual connection to Our Lady as the pivotal catalyst to their
earthly missions. St. Louis de Montfort was the first
to propose a formalized method for total consecration, but that is not to say that great Saints such as
St. Dominic, St. Francis of Assisi, and others did not
carry within them the promise of doing Our Lady's
bidding.

Another one of Our Lady's most beloved sons,
Pope St. John Paul II, would consecrate not only his
life to her, but also his papacy. Taking the motto
Totus Tuus (Totally Yours), he became Mary's humble servant, and throughout his life, he was able to
stop wars, heal souls, and even survive an assassina-
tion attempt, a nazi invasion of his native Poland,
and more spiritual torment than you and I could
ever imagine.

In his Apostolic Letter, *Rosarium Virginis
Mariae*, St. Pope John Paul II spoke about the importance of the Rosary and how it relates to total
consecration to Our Lord through Our Lady:

Following in the path of Christ, in whom man's path is 'recapitulated', revealed and redeemed, believers come face to face with the image of the true man. Contemplating Christ's birth, they learn of the sanctity of life; seeing the household of Nazareth, they learn the original truth of the family according to God's plan; listening to the Master in the mysteries of his public ministry, they find the light which leads them to enter the Kingdom of God; and following him on the way to Calvary, they learn the meaning of salvific suffering. Finally, contemplating Christ and his Blessed Mother in glory, they see the goal towards which each of us is called, if we allow ourselves to be healed and transformed by the Holy Spirit. It could be said that each mystery of the Rosary, carefully meditated, sheds light on the mystery of man...To pray the Rosary is to hand over our burdens to the merciful hearts of Christ and his Mother. (*RVM*, 25)

The Rosary, then, is our safety rope in times of trouble. On it, we place our burdens, our difficulties, and our needs so that our lives can be unknotted and straightened. Total consecration through the Rosary can thus create a singular spiritual connection to save us in our times of most desperate need and manifest God's love in our daily lives.

Many of us carry within us a soul that craves God beyond our otherwise stable lives. Others seek his presence in the depths of profound darkness. Regardless of our state in life, we make our way through our day-to-day responsibilities and, while we are satisfied with much of what we have become, we remain thirsty for something more, something outside of our individual abilities. In short, we long for holiness.

St. Pope John Paul II wrote,

> The Rosary does indeed 'mark the rhythm of human life', bringing it into harmony with the 'rhythm' of God's own life, in the joyful communion of the Holy Trinity, our life's destiny and deepest longing....The Rosary helps us to be conformed ever more closely to Christ until we attain true holiness. (*RVM*, 26)

And there, in the most intimate companion that ever was, the bond that, through Mary acting as the bridge between heaven and earth, brought us Jesus, true God and true Man, in whom we find the peace that our souls desire. St. Louis de Montfort once wrote, "Mary is the safest, easiest, shortest and most perfect way of approaching Jesus" (*True Devotion*). And it is this book's premise that the Rosary is the safest, easiest, shortest, and most perfect way of approaching Mary.

St. Pope John Paul II emphasizes this point:

Anyone who assimilates the mystery of Christ – and this is clearly the goal of the Rosary – learns the secret of peace and makes it his life's project. Moreover, by virtue of its meditative character, with the tranquil succession of Hail Marys, the Rosary has a peaceful effect on those who pray it, disposing them to receive and experience in their innermost depths, and to spread around them, that true peace which is the special gift of the Risen Lord. (cf. Jn 14:27; 20.21) (*RVM,* 40)

How This Consecration Works

There are several different methods by which one can consecrate him or herself to Jesus through Mary. Most take place over the course of a 33-day period, require a certain degree of penance, a daily examination of conscience, and a litany of prayers to be recited each day.

The method laid out in this book does all of those things, but it focuses primarily on the mysteries of the rosary. If you are not sure how to pray the rosary correctly, please turn to the appendix at the end of this book to learn how. The mysteries of the rosary are said on the following days:

Monday and Saturday – The Joyful Mysteries

Tuesday and Friday – The Sorrowful Mysteries

Thursday – The Luminous Mysteries

Sunday and Wednesday – The Glorious Mysteries

For a more detailed breakdown on why the mysteries are divided into these days, see the section entitled "Distribution Over Time" in the appendix.

For the 33 days in which you will be completing your Rosary Consecration, you will pray one set of the aforementioned mysteries for an entire week. Your schedule will look like this:

Week 1 – The Joyful Mysteries

Week 2 – The Luminous Mysteries

Week 3 – The Sorrowful Mysteries

Week 4 – The Glorious Mysteries

Week 5 – Pray the mysteries indicated at the end of each reflection

Day 1

The Joyful Mysteries

All men and women desire happiness. We are wired for it. From the first moments of our existence in our mother's womb to the moment of our deaths, we yearn for our physical, emotional, and ultimately our spiritual desires to be met. We are said to be *happy* when these needs are met and *sad* when they are not.

What we sometimes fail to recognize is that true happiness isn't achieved by man's efforts alone. True happiness cannot be achieved by man; it is only through the degree by which man serves God that his joy is given to him. St. Thomas Aquinas echoes this when he wrote, "The active life, which is busy with many things, has less of happiness than the contemplative life, which is busied with one thing, i.e. the contemplation of truth" (ST I-II q.3 a.2). Hence, the contemplative religious has an advantage when it comes to attaining happiness, for "[a]n unmarried woman or a virgin is anxious about the things of the Lord, so that she may be holy in both body and spirit. A married woman, on the other hand, is anxious about the things of the world, how she may please her husband" (1 Corinthians 7:34).

However, this doesn't exclude the lay man or woman from attaining happiness per se. In fact, St. Augustine once wrote, "Many men, who are great and worthy of imitation, have applied themselves to the study of wisdom in the marriage state." Holiness is for everyone insofar as we are able to live lives of constant contemplation; that is, in practicing the presence of God in thought, word, and act, we shall be happy.

The Joyful mysteries of the rosary provide us with a framework for achieving this end. In *Rosarium Virgins Marie*, St. Pope John Paul II describes the Joyful mysteries in the following way:

> The first five decades, the "joyful mysteries", are marked by the joy radiating from the event of the Incarnation. This is clear from the very first mystery, the Annunciation, where Gabriel's

greeting to the Virgin of Nazareth is linked to an invitation to messianic joy: "Rejoice, Mary". The whole of salvation history, in some sense the entire history of the world, has led up to this greeting. If it is the Father's plan to unite all things in Christ (cf. Eph 1:10), then the whole of the universe is in some way touched by the divine favour with which the Father looks upon Mary and makes her the Mother of his Son. The whole of humanity, in turn, is embraced by the fiat with which she readily agrees to the will of God.

Exultation is the keynote of the encounter with Elizabeth, where the sound of Mary's voice and the presence of Christ in her womb cause John to "leap for joy" (cf. Lk 1:44). Gladness also fills the scene in Bethlehem, when the birth of the divine Child, the Saviour of the world, is announced by the song of the angels and proclaimed to the shepherds as "news of great joy" (Lk 2:10).

The final two mysteries, while preserving this climate of joy, already point to the drama yet to come. The Presentation in the Temple not only expresses the joy of the Child's consecration and the ecstasy of the aged Simeon; it also records the prophecy that Christ will be a "sign of contradiction" for Israel and that a sword will pierce his mother's heart (cf Lk 2:34-35). Joy mixed with drama marks the fifth mystery, the finding of the twelve-year-old Jesus in the Temple. Here he appears in his divine wisdom as he listens and raises questions, already in effect one who "teaches". The revelation of his mystery as the Son wholly dedicated to his Father's affairs proclaims the radical nature of the Gospel, in which even the closest of human relationships are challenged by the absolute demands of the Kingdom. Mary and Joseph, fearful and anxious, "did not understand" his words (Lk 2:50).

To meditate upon the "joyful" mysteries, then, is to enter into the ultimate causes and the deepest meaning of Christian joy. It is to focus on the realism of the mystery of the Incarnation and on the obscure foreshadowing of the mystery of the saving Passion. Mary leads us to discover the secret of Christian joy, reminding us

that Christianity is, first and foremost, eu-
angelion, "good news", which has as its heart
and its whole content the person of Jesus Christ,
the Word made flesh, the one Saviour of the
world.

(*RVM*, 20)

Today, as you pray the Joyful Mysteries, contemplate the joy of the "Good News" in the person
of Jesus Christ, your closest brother, and Mary, your
spiritual mother.

Pray all of the Joyful Mysteries of the Rosary

Day 2

The Annunciation

"He who has the Son has life."

- 1 John 4:12

Who can say in literal truth that she had the Son of God within her, and thus the fullness of life, but Mary? She, who existed as an ideal in the mind of God, was greeted by the Angel Gabriel when he proclaimed "Hail, Mary," a greeting of royalty that not only surprised her, but confused her as well. According to scripture "she was greatly troubled at what was said and pondered what sort of greeting this might be" (Luke 1:29). After a brief conversation with the Angel, she made what is known as her "Fiat," or her "yes," to God.

In a similar way we, too, feel troubled when we walk down the aisle to receive the Eucharist during Mass. In the moment of the consecration, we become shadows of Mary, replicating for a brief moment her spiritual submission.

There are interesting parallels to Our Lady's final response to the Angel and our response to the Priest's *Ecce Agnus Dei* prayer. While we acknowledge our sinfulness and say "fiat" to God's will, Mary in her perfect grace altered her response to better suit her state — "Behold, I am the handmaid of the Lord. Be it done to me according to your word."

In each of these statements, there is a formula:

1. We admit our inferiority and accept our humility / fear of God.
2. We submit to His divine will.
3. We make an additional plea for mercy that *we* need, but Mary, being sinless, did not. Hence, we say, "Say the word and my soul shall be healed" whereas Mary didn't need to make such a statement. Instead, she was able to say simply, "Be it done to me."

At the sweet sound of Mary's "fiat," the Word was made flesh within her, and we became her spiritual Children from that moment on.

When we consciously and willfully humble our-selves before God and submit to his will, we honor her Divine Motherhood and follow her lead in our journey toward Christ. This call to holiness is a daily, even a moment-by-moment, occurrence. Every second of our lives is an Annunciation of sorts as our Creator uses nature, our intellect, and our will to call us to a closer union with Him.

But on the spiritual level, we relive that quiet night with Mary and Gabriel most intimately in the brief moments before accepting the Eucharist. May we be an echo of Our Lady's "fiat" so that we, too, can accept God into our bodies and souls. For "he who has the Son has life" (1 Jn. 4:12) and with God infused within your soul, your every action can be a reverberation of His call to holiness.

"The holy Spirit will come upon you, and the power of the Most High will overshadow you. Therefore the child to be born will be called holy, the Son of God."
- Luke 1:35

Pray all of the Joyful Mysteries of the Rosary

Day 3

The Visitation

"...those who hope in the Lord
will renew their strength.
They will soar on wings like eagles;
they will run and not grow weary,
they will walk and not be faint."

- Isaiah 40:31

When a man falls in love, there is an eagerness about him. He wants to go to sleep quickly in order to wake up to a new day with his beloved. She overtakes his mind and his plans for that day. All of his thoughts pull toward her like a magnet to iron. His work, his recreation, even his philosophical musings are all painted with the colors of her beauty and influence. He is smitten.

While he is away from her, however, he must wait in hopes of their next meeting. Waiting, of course, is a common thread of the fabric of life. Not only must lovers wait for their next date, but men and women of all walks of life must wait in line at the market, and thirsty children must wait in line at the drinking fountain after a summer day of playing at the park. Waiting, thus, becomes the great equalizer for all humanity because it is a penance we are all familiar with.

The childhood of Jesus, including the intimate moments Mary shared with him in his first trimesters of embryonic life, were marked by a heavy dose of mysterious waiting. From his conception to age 30 when he began his ministry, we know virtually nothing about Jesus' infancy, adolescence, and early adulthood. And now, during the precious moments of the Visitation, Our Lady felt his kicks, stretches, and even his hiccups within her womb. She, along with all of the souls to ever have existed both past and future, waited.

Her kinswoman, Elizabeth had had enough of waiting. When Mary's voice echoed into her home, the sound waves disrupted the silence of her soul. Immediately and without hesitation, she was spiritually awakened through Mary's words. Mary's vocal cords were the instrument through which the Word incarnate would reach out and enliven the spirit of Elizabeth.

Curiously enough, it wasn't just Elizabeth who heard His voice. John the Baptist, who was being knitted together in Elizabeth's womb, jumped for joy at the sound of Our Lady's greeting, too!

That same voice travels through eternity reverberating through souls at every minute of every day. In our daily lives, she calls out to us. In our interactions with others, she greets us. In our recreation and relaxation, she whispers our name. Even in our sleep, she meets us in our dreams.

Through Our Lady, God has called us to become one with him. We should be smitten and always thinking of him much like lovers who cannot function without the beloved at the forefront of their minds. And yet, there is a mystery about the whole process, a subliminal knowledge that we maintain as real, true, and good, almost all but hidden from our reality. We seek out this truth in our prayers, study, and throughout our day, but we never really conceptualize it in its entirety. Who is God? What does he want me to do? How will I do it? In short, we feel like we don't know exactly who we are or what we are supposed to do. We live in the same spiritual state of waiting that Mary, John, Elizabeth, and all of humanity did as Jesus remained "hidden" from us in his Mother's womb.

John the Baptist's period of patience came to an end much sooner than Elizabeth's who had waited her entire life to carry out her part in the mission of salvation. His thirst for truth was satiated in vitro while hers was granted through her pregnancy. Mary, who was no older than her early teens, waited patiently for the coming of her Son, her Savior, while he was constructed within her.

We who wait for the Lord do so with patience until the moment he becomes real to us. For some, this occurs earlier in life, like John the Baptist. For others, it takes longer, like Elizabeth. For all, however, the process remains mysterious, joyful, and filled with hope, but only if you have enough faith to recognize the sound of Our Lady's voice that surrounds your entire world, the same voice that surrounded Jesus' world while he was within her.

What the Visitation teaches us, then, is twofold:

1. True holiness requires patience.
2. When you hear her voice, you actually hear His.

"My soul proclaims the greatness of the Lord."

- Luke 1:46

Pray all of the Joyful Mysteries of the Rosary

Day 4

The Nativity

"When the angels went away from them to heaven, the shepherds said to one another, 'Let us go, then, to Bethlehem to see this thing that has taken place, which the Lord has made known to us.'"

- Luke 2:15

It is quiet. Silence embraces you with one arm and darkness the other. Your senses are heightened as you peer through the clouds to watch your flock. You are a shepherd on a mound above the bustling town of Bethlehem, which has finally quieted in the deep hours of the night. You are working in solace amongst the simplest of creatures. This evening isn't much different from every other normal evening, that is, until the silence is broken by a legion of angels who light up the sky and reverberate the sound waves announcing the birth of Christ is at hand.

As the story unfolds, the shepherds "make haste" to discover the Messiah's first moments of life outside of his mother's womb. They bow before him offering nothing but their simplistic lifestyle, company, and joy. They were the first among others with greater titles and esteem to witness Jesus in that stable, and the reason why they were given such an honor was likely because of their dedication to silence.

Their story parallels the Annunciation to Mary. Our Lady, too, was given the news of Christ's arrival in the silence of her home. She, too, "made haste" to respond to God's request when she said "fiat" to his will. She, too, became one with the mystery of the incarnation as did the shepherds who welcomed him with their simplicity. She, too, was called to be an integral character in the story of salvation.

God speaks to us in the silence of our hearts. Our lives are filled with noise. We are constantly on the go. We have work responsibilities, home responsibilities, hobbies, parish events, goals, dreams, prayer time, and some of us even find ways to get sleeping and eating into that already crammed schedule. Not all of us can live the life of the shepherd or the cloistered religious whose sole existence is set in the foundation of constant contemplation and silent meditation. How glorious it would be if we could be like Mary and the Shepherds, blessed enough to experience the beauty of silence in the presence of the Christ child!

Mary understood this to the greatest degree when her Son was delivered into the world as a healthy baby boy. The shepherds experienced this second-hand as the first witnesses of Jesus' earthly mission to call all to himself. We experience this closeness when we encounter Jesus in the silence of our hearts through consistent and intentional daily prayer.

The rosary is the method *par excellence* toward discovering the mysteries of Christ. It is the means through which all people, regardless of their intellectual abilities, can enter into the person of Jesus Christ. The highly-educated doctor of philosophy is on the same spiritual wavelength as the poor beggar child when they wrap Our Lady's beads around their fingers. It doesn't matter if you pray in the middle of rush hour in the biggest city or on a lonely meadow in the middle of nowhere, attach yourself to her quiet heart and you will sit upon her lap, the Seat of all Wisdom.

The possibility of entering into a state of contemplative silence is very much possible for us. Our Lord, Our Lady, and the shepherds were able to do it in the hustle and bustle of Bethlehem during the busyness of the census. So, too, must we enter into the depths of silent contemplation during the hustle and bustle of our daily lives. We are a modern day Bethlehem, and in us the Lord has decided that he will make his dwelling. We simply need to find a silent place for him and for Our Lady to call "home."

"My dwelling place will be with them; I will be their God, and they will be my people."

- Ezekiel 37:27

Pray all of the Joyful Mysteries of the Rosary

Day 5

The Presentation

"He came in the Spirit into the temple; and when the parents brought in the child Jesus to perform the custom of the law in regard to him, he took him into his arms and blessed God, saying, 'Now, Master, you may let your servant go in peace, according to your word, for my eyes have seen your salvation, which you prepared in sight of all the peoples, a light for revelation to the Gentiles, and glory for your people Israel.'"

- Luke 2:27-32

You have a plan for your life. You have everything you desire mapped out in your mind, and you likely already know the steps you need to take in order to make it a reality. You might be studying to achieve your degree, working to earn a promotion, praying to discern your vocation, or planning for your retirement. Whatever your five-year plan is, however, God might have something else, something better, planned for your life.

Simeon had an experience like this. Here was a man who was given a divine revelation earlier in his life that he would see the Messiah before he died. Can you imagine what his daily life would have been like? He likely woke up every day thinking, "Today might be the day!" Both as a Rabbi and a man with such a promise, you would think that he'd spend his entire life inside the temple waiting for the revelation to take place.

And yet we find him away from the Temple, wrapped up in the goings on of his daily life when, all of a sudden, the Spirit entered his consciousness, and led him to the Temple. There, his gaze fell upon the God-man Jesus for whom his life had been lived as a constant sacrifice of hope.

Our mystical plans in life are limited by our incomplete knowledge of what we are capable of becoming. We are characters in the story of salvation, not the authors. When we make spiritual plans, it is akin to Odysseus penning the *Odyssey* instead of Homer telling it for him. Granted, we are given the grace to plan our lives in many ways that can add to spiritual flourishing (physical training, economic stability, intellectual achievement, etc.), but when it comes to the development of our souls, it would do us well to let God create within us the masterpiece that exists in his mind.

Who better to teach us how to empty ourselves of our own ambitions than Mary? Archbishop Fulton J. Sheen calls her "God's dream," and the "ideal that existed in God since the beginning of time." She is "the Ideal Woman," a perfect example of how faith coincides with grace. It is through her, the flawless vessel, that the epitome of perfection, God Himself, would come. It is also through her that all of God's children have their spiritual adoption.

We find this true not only in logic, but also in Scripture. In the book of Revelation, Our Lady is the primary target of Satan in the mystical battle for spiritual conquest. In chapter 12, it reads: "Then the dragon became angry with the woman and went off to wage war against the rest of her offspring, those who keep God's commandments and bear witness to Jesus" (Revelation 12:17).

We are the offspring of Our Lady. Our recitation of the Rosary binds us more closely to her and forges within us the bonds of love for her Son. She unites us to His will through every bead and teaches us how to empty ourselves of all that keeps us from achieving our ultimate goal: true happiness in this life and the next through Christ.

If you are still reading this book, you, like Simeon and Mary, have been led by the Spirit toward a closer encounter with Christ. Prompted by the holy Spirit, we, too, achieve all that we truly desire when we give up our own plans, consecrating ourselves to Jesus through Mary.

"But seek first his kingdom and his righteousness, and all these things will be given to you as well."

- Matthew 6:33

Pray all of the Joyful Mysteries of the Rosary

Day 6

The Finding of Jesus in the Temple

"Each year his parents went to Jerusalem for the feast of
Passover, and when he was twelve years old, they went
up according to festival custom. After they had
completed its days, as they were returning, the boy Jesus
remained behind in Jerusalem, but his parents did not
know it."

- Luke 2:41-43

I was once asked to tell which of the mysteries of
the rosary were the hardest for me to pray. The person asking the question was expecting me to say the
Sorrowful mysteries because, let's face it, they are
without a doubt the most terrifying, violent, and
saddening. But, to his surprise, I responded by saying the Joyful Mysteries were the most difficult to
pray. There is a certain darkness that overshadows
them that makes it hard to focus on their namesake
of "joy," especially if you put yourself in Mary's sandals.

In the Annunciation, she is asked to become the Mother of God. During the Visitation she travels to her cousin's home and back again while pregnant and alone. At the Nativity, she makes the perilous journey to Bethlehem at full term and cannot find a safe place for the Son of God to be born until the very last minute. During the Presentation, Simeon tells her that a sword will pierce her heart. And in the Finding of Jesus in the Temple, she experiences one of the most sorrowful moments of her life — losing Jesus. Indeed, the Joyful mysteries are wrapped in a mantle of darkness.

This final mystery puts an exclamation point on the worry and anxiety that only the Mother of God could endure. Her loss of God is akin to what St. John of the Cross calls our "dark night of the soul" in which he speaks of one's abandonment to self and the acceptance of living on God's pure grace. The final stanza reads:

I abandoned and forgot myself,
laying my face on my Beloved;
all things ceased; I went out from myself,

leaving my cares
forgotten among the lilies.

Our Lady experienced this total abandonment in her agonizing vexation over the loss of her Son. It is one of her many sorrows as well as ours to a lesser degree. While we have never "seen God" in the same way that she did, we experience a perceived lack of his presence in our lives and long for him all the more. That is what makes her loss far more devastating than our own, for she was Jesus' most loyal follower, his perfect servant, and if anyone was due to receive his most abundant graces of safety, assurance, and peace, it was her. And yet, he gave her no such gifts. On the contrary, she suffered anguish, pain, and loss due to the mystery of evil and suffering in a fallen world.

The secret of Christian holiness is not found in the joy that sparks from our virtue. Rather, it is forged in the difficult journey that ends in God's grace. Jesus told us that if we truly desired to be his disciples, that we must deny ourselves, pick up our crosses and follow him (Matthew 16:24).

Accomplishing this task requires that we pass through intense struggles in order to arrive at a pure, holy joy. If we are successful at living a Christian life, we will be given the graces of pain and suffering, which St. Mother Theresa calls "the kiss of Jesus – a sign that you have come so close to Him that He can kiss you."

It is through these trials and tribulations that Our Lady walked to the highest degree. She is the perfect model to imitate and the greatest of all counselors. Her love for humanity is expressed through the direct link that is her Rosary, which combines the harrowing trials and tribulations with the source of Christian joy. It is a paradox that reminds us that what we truly seek is God, who can be found not only in his presence, but also in his absence.

Upon returning to the temple, Mary and Joseph found Jesus among the teachers and rabbis learning from them and asking questions. They were astonished and said,

> "Son, why have you done this to us? Your father and I have been looking for you with great anxiety."

And he said to them, "Why were you looking for me?
Did you not know that I must be in my Father's house?"
But they did not understand what he said to them.

- Luke 2:48-50

It is ok to not understand God. It is ok to find
yourself in the difficulties that life presents. It is ok
to feel lost, disillusioned, and utterly hopeless in
your efforts to search for God. In fact, *that* is the perfect place to find him, for it is our most difficult moments that he is closest to us on the cross.

"If we are afflicted, it is for your encouragement and
salvation; if we are encouraged, it is for your encouragement, which enables you to endure the same sufferings
that we suffer."

- 2 Corinthians 1:6

Pray all of the Joyful Mysteries of the Rosary

Day 7

Mary's Divine Motherhood

Mary is the *Theotokos*, which is the Greek word meaning the "God bearer" or the "Birth-giver of God." It is through her that God chose to enter into our world in the form of Jesus Christ, who took from Our Lady the life-giving threads that would join both God and man into one being. Mary's divine motherhood, then, has its source in Jesus, who defines her and the vital role she plays in the story of salvation.

The official dogma of Mary's divine motherhood was proclaimed at the Council of Ephesus in 431, where it was written: "If anyone does not confess that God is truly Emmanuel, and that on this account the Holy Virgin is the Mother of God (for according to the flesh she gave birth to the Word of God become flesh by birth), let him be anathema."

The Catechism of the Catholic Church goes into further detail:

"Called in the Gospels 'the mother of Jesus,' Mary is acclaimed by Elizabeth, at the prompting of the Spirit and even before the birth of her son, as 'the mother of my Lord.' In fact, the One whom she conceived as man by the Holy Spirit, who truly became her Son according to the flesh, was none other than the Father's eternal Son, the second person of the Holy Trinity. Hence the Church confesses that Mary is truly 'Mother of God' (Theotokos)." (*CCC*, 495)

God chose to come through Mary in the fullness of time to provide redemption for humanity. That's why it is of great importance that we recognize that Christology and Mariology are interconnected. When one gets Christ's role wrong, one also gets Mary's role wrong and visa-versa. If one sees Jesus as only man, then it is easy for one to underestimate Mary's importance and claim that she was no more than a fleshly conduit through which a regular man named Jesus came to us. This dilutes the importance of both and puts them on the same existential plane as you and me.

Another false claim is that Jesus had two distinct natures, one human and one Divine, and Mary was simply the means through which his "human" side came to be. This also denies the true essence of who Jesus is — one Divine Person in whom two natures, the divine and human, are united.

And with this belief in Christ's dual nature, which is referred to as his *hypostatic* union, one must also accept Mary's proper title as the Mother of God. She can be known by no other name, for she was chosen to give birth to the second person in the Trinity, Jesus Christ, who is both God and man. Hence, St. John tells us that Jesus is "the Word made flesh" (John 1:14) and consequently "the Word was God" (John 1:1); thus, Mary is the mother of the Word, and so she is rightly the Mother of God.

Some might ask if Jesus underwent change when His divinity became flesh. The truth is that it wasn't God who underwent change, but man!

St. Thomas Aquinas explains:

"Since the Divine Person is infinite, no addition can be made to it. Hence Cyril says (Cyril of

Ephesus, Part 1, chapter 26): 'We do not conceive the mode of conjunction to be according
to addition: just as in the union of man with
God, nothing is added to God by the grace of
adoption, but what is Divine is united to man;
hence, not God but man is perfected.'"

When God became man in Jesus Christ, He provided us with the possibility of becoming like him,
like *God*. In the mystery of the Incarnation, man was
given a metric through which we were able to
achieve the highest potential of our being. St. John
teaches us that, "We are God's children now; what
we shall be has not yet been revealed. We do know
that when it is revealed we shall be like him, for we
shall see him as he is" (1 John 3:2). Our lives, then,
are in a constant *becoming*, a series of events that
molds us into union with God so as to "be perfect,
just as [God] is perfect" (Matthew 5:48).

In the Joyful mysteries, we see the two souls who
lived out this perfection from the moment of their
conception until their glorious resurrection. Jesus,
who was both God and man, received his life from

his most humble and loyal servant, Mary. It is also through Mary that we receive *our* union with Jesus, for in becoming his brothers and sisters, we thus become sons and daughters to his mother. When we recognize Our Lady as the Mother of God, we join the angels and Saints in an unending hymn of praise in which all generations call her "Blessed among women."

Today, as you pray the Joyful mysteries, recall that mysterious union shared between the dark moments and happy moments of life. May you tread through the hills and valleys of your spiritual journey with the company of Jesus and Mary who protect us in the shadows and walk with us toward the light of peace.

Pray all of the Joyful Mysteries of the Rosary

Day 8

The Luminous Mysteries

Jesus told the people, "I am the light of the world. Whoever follows me will not walk in darkness, but will have the light of life."

- John 8:12

In the Luminous mysteries of the Rosary, we become witnesses to this eternal light and, to the degree of grace we are given, we are able to reflect it in our own lives.

This ability to spread the light of Jesus is crystalized in our evangelistic efforts. To be "luminous" in this dark world, we imitate Our Lord by becoming like him in every possible way. This includes becoming his adopted son or daughter in the waters of Baptism, pursuing our missionary vocation to serve the needs of our communities, preaching the Good News in both word and deed, contemplating the glory of God, and celebrating the Holy Sacrifice of the Mass each week. These steps are laid out by Jesus as the foundational structure to our living a holy life in the Luminous mysteries.

In *Rosarium Virgins Marie*, St. Pope John Paul II describes the Luminous mysteries in the following way:

> Moving on from the infancy and the hidden life in Nazareth to the public life of Jesus, our contemplation brings us to those mysteries which may be called in a special way "mysteries of light". Certainly the whole mystery of Christ is a mystery of light. He is the "light of the world" (Jn 8:12). Yet this truth emerges in a special way during the years of his public life, when he proclaims the Gospel of the Kingdom. In proposing to the Christian community five significant moments — "luminous" mysteries — during this phase of Christ's life, I think that the following can be fittingly singled out: (1) his Baptism in the Jordan, (2) his self-manifestation at the wedding of Cana, (3) his proclamation of the Kingdom of God, with his call to conversion, (4)

his Transfiguration, and finally, (5) his institution of the Eucharist, as the sacramental expression of the Paschal Mystery.

Each of these mysteries is a revelation of the Kingdom now present in the very person of Jesus. The Baptism in the Jordan is first of all a mystery of light. Here, as Christ descends into the waters, the innocent one who became "sin" for our sake (cf. 2 Cor 5:21), the heavens open wide and the voice of the Father declares him the beloved Son (cf. Mt 3:17 and parallels), while the Spirit descends on him to invest him with the mission which he is to carry out. Another mystery of light is the first of the signs, given at Cana (cf. Jn 2:1- 12), when Christ changes water into wine and opens the hearts of the disciples to faith, thanks to the intervention of Mary, the first among believers. Another mystery of light is the preaching by which Jesus proclaims the coming of the Kingdom of God, calls to conversion (cf. Mk 1:15) and forgives the sins of all who draw near to him in humble trust (cf. Mk 2:3-13; Lk 7:47- 48): the inauguration of that ministry of mercy which he continues to exercise until the end of the world, particularly through the Sacrament of Reconciliation which he has entrusted to his Church (cf. Jn 20:22-23). The mystery of light par excellence is the Transfiguration, traditionally believed to have taken place on Mount Tabor. The glory of the Godhead shines forth from the face of Christ as the Father commands the astonished Apostles to "listen to him" (cf. Lk 9:35 and parallels) and to prepare to experience with him the agony of the Passion, so as to come with him to the joy of the Resurrection and a life transfigured by the Holy Spirit. A final mystery of light is the institution of the Eucharist, in which Christ offers his body and blood as food under the signs of bread and wine, and testifies "to the end" his love for humanity (Jn 13:1), for whose salvation he will offer himself in sacrifice.

In these mysteries, apart from the miracle at Cana, the presence of Mary remains in the background. The Gospels make only the briefest reference to her occasional presence at one moment or other during the preaching of Jesus (cf. Mk 3:31-5; Jn 2:12), and they give no indication that she was present at the Last Supper and the institution of the Eucharist. Yet the role she assumed at Cana in some way accompanies Christ throughout his ministry. The revelation made directly by the Father at the Baptism in the Jordan and echoed by John the Baptist is placed upon Mary's lips at Cana, and it becomes the great maternal counsel which Mary addresses to the Church of every age: "Do whatever he tells you" (Jn 2:5). This counsel is a fitting introduction to the words and signs of Christ's public ministry and it forms the Marian foundation of all the "mysteries of light".

(RVM, 21)

As you pray the Luminous mysteries each day this week, focus your contemplative thought on Jesus' ministry. As you delve into his methods, consider the ways in which he calls you to bring light into the world.

Pray all of the Luminous Mysteries of the Rosary

Day 9

The Baptism of Our Lord in the Jordan River

"Then Jesus came from Galilee to John at the Jordan
to be baptized by him."

- Matthew 3:13

Jesus told us that we are the light of the world. He said, "Your light must shine before others, that they may see your good deeds and glorify your heavenly Father" (Matthew 5:16). In this first mystery of light, or luminous mystery, he beckons us to be that light, to let it shine more brightly than we could possibly imagine, or even attempt, through our own efforts.

In order to accomplish that task, however, we must first be *formed*. John the Baptist spent the majority of his life in the solitude of the desert wearing camel's hair and eating locusts and wild honey. He lived amongst the hermits of the Judean desert who taught him the Jewish religion. He was called not to become a professor, but a prophet, and in following

God's voice in the silence of the desert, he became the audible voice of reason to a fallen generation.

Jesus was also well-formed. Instead of living the life of an hermit, isolated from society, he was woven into the tapestry of his community by the thread of his family. His father taught him the life skills of manual labor, which allowed Jesus to understand the fruits of his people's daily work. Additionally, Our Lady watched over him as a quintessential caregiver. She not only took care of the household, but she also nurtured Jesus' mind and body, thus helping him develop divine wisdom and providing him with physical nourishment.

As a result of this dual formation between John the Baptist and Jesus, the two met in the Jordan River to inaugurate Jesus' ministry. Jesus was immersed into the waters so that he could emerge as the light-bearing servant through which humanity would be saved. In doing so, he provided us a bridge through which our own acts of virtue would work as a mirror of his love and reflect his celestial light toward mankind. This bridge is known as the sacrament of Baptism.

Through our baptism, we follow Christ's example and trail-blaze new acts in new territories where his love is needed. Thus, we are also immersed in modern missionary work by constantly seeking out people where they are at and by preparing the way of the Lord, just like John the Baptist.

How do you do this? You go where the people are, and you serve them. Before Jesus took his first steps in his ministry, John the Baptist had been preparing the way for his arrival. His preaching and baptizing gathered together all who had desired to repent from their sinful ways, thus kindling the flame through which Jesus would light their souls on fire. People would come from all over to be baptized by water at the hands of John, and when Jesus took the torch, many of John's disciples began to follow him. The light of Christ baptized them in the fire of his love, and that flame would eventually spread throughout the entire world.

Today, that torch is carried by the children of Mary. Our mission is the same as Jesus' and John the Baptist's, namely, to be formed by the guidance of Our Lady and to become a voice in the desert that will guide God's people along the path of peace. We are the torchbearers of salvation who light the way for all to follow Christ toward their final destination — the salvation of their souls and the eternal joy that comes with it.

"I am baptizing you with water, for repentance, but the one who is coming after me is mightier than I. I am not worthy to carry his sandals. He will baptize you with the holy Spirit and fire."

- Matthew 3:11

Pray all of the Luminous Mysteries of the Rosary

Day 10

The Miracle at the Wedding at Cana

When the wine ran short, the mother of Jesus said
to him, "They have no wine." [And] Jesus said to her,
"Woman, how does your concern affect me? My hour
has not yet come." His mother said to the servers, "Do
whatever he tells you."

- John 2:3-5

There are three missions described in the mystery of the Miracle at the Wedding at Cana. First, there is the mission of the married couple whose vocation to marriage made the celebration possible. Second, there's the mission of Mary whose service was to ensure that all who came would be satisfied with food and drink. Finally, there was the mission of Jesus who, at the request of his Mother, would produce his first miracle and thus begin his public ministry.

The first mission is one that most can connect with. We've all been to weddings, and we witness many married couples in our daily lives. This mystery proves that the vocation to marriage is one of great importance to God, for it is in the context of this fundamental unit of societal love that both his Son and Our Lady are ever present. In every marriage, Our Lord and Our Lady call no attention to themselves, but rather they quietly serve the needs of both husband and wife so that both can be satisfied with the necessary graces to truly love one another selflessly.

The second mission proves that God has given Mary a special ability of knowing the needs of the souls around her and the special grace of direct intercession with her Son. And how could Jesus deny his mother's requests? Together, Mary keeps busy seeking out the needs of others while Jesus honors her devotion to souls by granting her every request to save them.

Interestingly enough, in Jesus' mission of this mystery, he tells his mother, "Woman, how does your concern affect me?" His use of the term *Woman* is not a crass insult we take it to be on a first read, but rather it is the highest compliment Jesus could give her; when he called her "woman," he enthroned her as *the* woman of all women. This is why we pray "Blessed are you among women," when we pray the hail Mary, because in this instant, Jesus affirmed Mary's place as the "New Eve," the matriarch of his New Covenant who would become the "Mother of all Christians" (Rev. 12:17).

Jesus then tells her "My hour has not yet come." This was not a statement, but a request. In his words, he asks Mary to look deep into her heart and decide, "Is this what you really want?" The two have been inseparable since the day of his conception. The most perfect beings to have ever existed lived with one another in perfect peace for 30 years, and now, Mary has asked her Son to begin his mission. Both know that this will result in the most agonizing sorrows of their lives. Simeon told them this much during the Presentation in the Temple saying, "Behold, this child is destined for the fall and rise of many in Israel, and to be a sign that will be contradicted! (and you yourself a sword will pierce) so that the thoughts of many hearts may be revealed" (Luke 2:34). Hence, he speaks to her soul and essentially says, "Are you ready for what is to come?" Mary responds with her final words recorded in the Bible: "Do whatever he tells you."

Our mission is the same. We must be prepared to leave our comfort zones. We must be willing to travel the long and arduous journey of proclaiming Jesus Christ in our daily lives. We cannot do it alone, which is why Mary remains beside us, constantly seeking out our needs and bringing them to her Son as prayers of intercession. Together, we relive the intimate conversation between Jesus and his mother and ask ourselves at every moment, "Are we ready for what is to come?"

Come what may, if we remain faithful, we are guaranteed three things: the strength to endure whatever sufferings will come, the intercession of Our Lady who bestows upon us the graces necessary for our salvation, and the miracles of God who takes the flavorless water jugs of our lives and turns them into the finest of all wines.

Are you ready for that?

"Everyone serves good wine first, and then when people
have drunk freely, an inferior one; but you have kept
the good wine until now."

- John 2:10

Pray all of the Luminous Mysteries of the Rosary

Day 11

The Proclamation of the Kingdom

"But seek first the kingdom [of God] and his
righteousness, and all these things will be given
you besides."

- Matthew 6:33

You have been given a mission by God. It is a
mission that is unique only to you. You alone have
been given the talents, the knowledge, and the will
to complete it. Here's the problem – No one can tell
you what yours is. In fact, it is very likely that you
also do not know exactly what it is that God has
called you to do.

And that is ok... for now. During his ministry,
Jesus' primary mission was to proclaim the Kingdom of God in both word and deed. He filled the
airwaves with his words and miracles so that the
hearts of the people he preached to would be moved
toward virtue. As a result, his words remain in our
own hearts today as they echo through our souls in

hopes that we, too, will receive his graces and attain our salvation.

Interestingly enough, Jesus charged us to become partakers in his same mission of saving souls. He told us to "Go," and to "make disciples of all nations, baptizing them in the name of the Father, and of the Son, and of the holy Spirit, teaching them to observe all that [he has] commanded [us]" (Matthew 28:19-20). To add height to his already high expectations for us, he said, "So be perfect, just as your heavenly Father is perfect" (Matthew 5:48).

That is kind of a tall order... But it doesn't stop there. With his challenge, Jesus also gave us a promise. He said, "I will be with you always until the end of the age" (Matthew 28:20). On top of that, he gave us motivation to eradicate our flaws through our own preaching. He told us, "Whoever turns a sinner from the error of their way will save them from death and cover over a multitude of sins" (James 5:20). In other words, the ministry in which we partake for the salvation of souls will not only save others, but it will also help save our own lives by canceling out all of the sins that condemn us.

We aren't perfect. It seems illogical that God would send us, as broken as we are, to proclaim the Kingdom. Who are we but weak sinners to carry out the will of God by preaching and serving others like he did? In truth, we are nothing alone. But with God we become something greater.

The book of Hebrews states, "Jesus offered one sacrifice for sins and took his seat forever at the right hand of God; now he waits until his enemies are placed beneath his feet. By one offering he has forever perfected those who *are being* sanctified" (Hebrews 10:12-14). While we are imperfect in our humanity, we are currently being perfected by the grace of God to the degree in which we pursue him. Faith manifests itself in love, and the output of our love is what builds up our sanctification.

You are being built into a "spiritual house" on which the foundation is that of the apostles and Mary with Christ as the cornerstone (1 Peter 2:4-5). All you have to do is contemplate the mission that God has given you to complete, then strive relentlessly to fulfill it.

That is why the proclamation of the Kingdom is so important to our own sense of mission. When we read Christ's words in Scripture, we mystically *attain* his word as it manifests itself in our hearts. It is a living word, a *logos*, that enlivens us and gives us clarity in thought, strength in virtue, and sage wisdom. These are the same traits of all the Saints who, when they heard the voice of God, responded to it.

Proclaiming God's Kingdom is a mission that takes a lifetime to complete. We will never know if we are doing it perfectly until the day when we enter heaven and look down upon the final earthy product of our labors. Then, when we, too, exist beyond space and time, we will look at our lives through God's eternal vision and become the perfect version of ourselves, the one God meant for us to be.

"...the Lord ordered that those who preach the gospel should live by the gospel."

- 1 Corinthians 9:14

Pray all of the Luminous Mysteries of the Rosary

Day 12

The Transfiguration

"After six days Jesus took Peter, James, and John his brother, and led them up a high mountain by themselves. And he was transfigured before them; his face shone like the sun and his clothes became white as light."

- Matthew 17:1-2

We long for something more than what we currently have. St. Augustine expressed this unquenchable desire when he said, "Lord, we are restless until we rest in you." All of us seek a certain greatness that is beyond us, a glimpse of the eternal, a satiating of our thirst for the divine.

The Transfiguration is the mystery of light par excellence. Jesus takes Peter, James, and John away from the normalcy of their lives and leads them up the mountain to experience the foretelling of what is to come of his part in the story of salvation — namely, his glorified body.

At the top of the mountain, he stood amongst them in dazzling white and blinding light. At his side stood Moses and Elijah, two Jewish prophets whose presence confirmed that Jesus was the completion of the Old Law. His authority over the entire world was yet again confirmed when, from the sky came God's voice saying, "This is my beloved Son with whom I am well pleased. Listen to him."

Peter asked of Our Lord during this spectacle if he should create tents for Jesus, Moses, and Elijah. In doing so, he tried to box God into the level of humanity. He attempted to place such glory and power into a small tent to be hidden from the world. What an ordinary response to such an extraordinary event! Jesus is the light of the world, and according to the Psalmist "in [his] light we see light."

There are only three "boxes" in which Jesus accepted to be confined in during his life; the first was the womb of Our Lady through which he became man and the light of the world. The other was the tomb through which the light of his resurrection saved all mankind from their sin. The third is the tabernacle in which the light of the Eucharist shines graces upon those who receive him in Holy Communion.

It is our responsibility to pursue the light of truth with sincerity of heart. Like the tortoise and the hare, we either seek out Our Lord in haste, or we are slow and steady during this race toward our salvation. Unfortunately for many, we stop all too soon for breaks in between, and we end up in the darkness of our own weaknesses. The result is a retreat to self which shadows our light so the world cannot see it. We become dim in our spirituality, and we place God in our little boxes afraid to let him out because we don't want to trust him with the outcome of our own life decisions.

If you are longing for holiness and the greatness that comes with it, then it is your responsibility to pursue the light of truth with the capacity of the hare and the consistency of the tortoise. With Mary as your companion and Jesus as your guide, you are better fit to climb the mountain of salvation and thus be transfigured into the fullness of your potential. Perhaps it would do us well to consider that Peter's physical tents made of wood and animal skins could never suffice for the "Light of the World." On the contrary, our very bodies, which are temples of the holy Spirit, could satisfy Christ's thirst for your soul.

As you reflect on the Luminous mysteries today, consider all of the ways you place God into a box. Then, let him out. Let him out of the one's *you* create, and into the one *He* created in you.

> "My soul, be at rest in God alone,
> from whom comes my hope."
>
> - Psalm 62:6

Pray all of the Luminous Mysteries of the Rosary

Day 13

The Institution of the Eucharist

"While they were eating, Jesus took bread, said the blessing, broke it, and giving it to his disciples said, 'Take and eat; this is my body.'"

- Matthew 26:26

Modern science has discovered that the cells of a woman's baby remain within her physiology for decades after her baby is born. The term for these remaining cells is called *microchimera*. Biologists have many theories about how these cells affect the woman ranging from effects such as better wound healing to protection from Alzheimer's. This microchimera proves that a woman's child accounts for much more than just mere relationship — the very fiber of her being has her child's DNA sewn into her own in a mystical, physiological phenomenon.

If this is true among the sons of Adam and daughters of Eve, imagine the biological connection between the New Adam, Jesus, and the New Eve, his

Mother, Mary. The Bible mentions several instances
of how people were affected by Jesus' touch. One
man was healed of leprosy, another man of blindness, a woman from severe hemorrhages. All of
these were, indeed, positive, but what of the Mother
of Our Lord who, by all scientific logic, maintained
within her perpetually the actual cells of God? What
did she receive?

Apart from being "full of grace," she also received a "sword to the heart." The benefit of being
filled with Christ's lifeblood was that the former
overshadowed the latter, and she was able to heroi-
cally endure the sorrows that would have destroyed
anyone else who had to confront them without the
aid of grace.

The Institution of the Eucharist was God's way
of providing us with the graces necessary to endure
our own sorrows. Through his life-giving words at
the Last Supper, Jesus gave to us the opportunity to
become "full of Grace" on a visceral, biological level.
He commanded that we eat his body and drink his
blood and in doing so he bestowed upon us the very
microchimera that dwelled within Mary.

The Eucharist, although it is true food and true drink, is not regarded so much for its biological properties, but rather for its spiritual impact. Jesus told his followers, "I am the living bread that came down from heaven; whoever eats this bread will live forever; and the bread that I will give is my flesh for the life of the world" (John 6:51). Many took his words for their biological implications saying, "How can this man give us [his] flesh to eat?" (John 6:52). Had they heard his words with their souls, they would have understood him when he said, "Amen, amen, I say to you, unless you eat the flesh of the Son of Man and drink his blood, you do not have life within you. Whoever eats my flesh and drinks my blood has eternal life, and I will raise him on the last day" (John 6:53-54).

The Eucharist is the microchimera of our bodies, but it is the MACROchimera of our souls. *The Catechism of the Catholic Church* refers to it as "the source and summit of the Christian life" (*CCC*, 1324), and, as such, it is our privilege and responsibility to receive Our Lord's body, blood, soul, and divinity with a pure heart and a clean soul.

At the Last Supper, it is likely that many of Jesus' closest disciples were utterly confused at his words. Perhaps we, too, are confused by the mystery of transubstantiation and our unworthiness of accepting the Eucharist. But Mary must have understood with her infused knowledge from the spirit Christ's true presence in the bread and wine. Allow her to teach you that intimate mystery as you meditate upon this mystery of her most holy rosary today.

"I am the bread of life; whoever comes to me will never hunger, and whoever believes in me will never thirst."

- John 6:35

Pray all of the Luminous Mysteries of the Rosary

Day 14

The Immaculate Conception

Pope Pius IX, in his Apostolic Constitution *Ineffabilis Deus,* declared "that the most Blessed Virgin Mary, from the first moment of her conception, by a singular grace and privilege from Almighty God and in view of the merits of Jesus Christ, was kept free of every stain of original sin." This is what is meant by the Immaculate Conception – that through a very special grace Mary never sinned and was thus able to become the Mother of God.

As mentioned on day seven, Mary is the *Theotokos* or "God bearer." The Immaculate Conception, then, is a dogma that is meant to honor Jesus more than it honors Mary. Many people tend to think that Mary's Immaculate Conception deifies her, but nothing is further from the truth. On the contrary, this dogma preserves a unique holiness that is only given to the person of Jesus. The fact that Mary was sinless provides no promise for her deification, but the *magnification* of *Christ's* divinity.

Imagine there is an abyss into which each and every man and woman to ever exist are blinded from and, due to their blindness, they all fall into the abyss. All humans are victims of what we call original sin, represented by the blindness of our race. This original sin is passed down from Adam and Eve to all humanity and, as a result, we gather together in the mystical abyss of personal and collective sinfulness.

However, Jesus came down to cure the blindness of men and remove their original sin. For most of us, he waits until we have already fallen into the abyss in order to catch us before we fall completely into the consuming fires. When we go to confession and confess our sins, it is like Jesus lifts us out of the abyss and puts our feet on firm ground to continue the journey toward eternal life in heaven. This is the process of salvation for every human being for all... all except one.

Mary was also in need of a Savior as she was in her humanity susceptible to original sin just like you and me. The difference, however, is that God saved her from falling into the abyss. He removed her blindness and, because of this grace, she maintained her perfection from the moment of her conception. It was only in this way that she could be "full of grace" so that she, and only she, could bear the perfect God and give him to the world.

The Catechism of the Catholic Church states, "To become the mother of the Savior, Mary 'was enriched by God with gifts appropriate to such a role.' The angel Gabriel at the moment of the annunciation salutes her as 'full of grace.' In fact, in order for Mary to be able to give the free assent of her faith to the announcement of her vocation, it was necessary that she be wholly borne by God's grace" (*CCC*, 490).

It was through the grace of the Immaculate Conception that Mary stands in stark contrast to Eve who brought sin into the world. Mary, then, is the "New Eve" through which sin is vanquished through Jesus, the "New Adam." It was through Mary's steadfast obedience and complete submission to God's will that she remains not only in constant unity with Jesus, but also with the entire Trinity and all creation.

It follows then that through Mary the spark of faith is ignited in every human heart as a kindling for the greater fire of God's love. Together, Jesus and Mary illumine our souls with the light of faith which, as you've seen, is on full display not only in the Luminous mysteries, but also in the dogma of the Immaculate Conception.

Pray all of the Luminous Mysteries of the Rosary

Day 15

The Sorrowful Mysteries

Too often, we tend to associate the word *love* with its emotional connotations. We rationalize what we want love to be based on how things and people make us feel. We "love" a thing or a person only insomuch as they appease our appetites for pleasure. Once they are unable to satisfy, they are abandoned, and we are left with only ourselves and our guilt.

Love, however, has a distinct denotative meaning. Love is a great sacrifice. It takes pain and suffering to realize the furthest limits of love. That's why Jesus tells us, "No one has greater love than this, to lay down one's life for one's friends" (John 15:13).

In the Sorrowful mysteries, we witness Jesus experience the greatest trials ever faced by a man to prove his love. He was slandered, ridiculed, beaten, spat upon, tortured, bamboozled, humiliated, deprived, deceived, ignored, and killed in the presence of his own mother. He went through all of the pain so that it could later be written, "...we do not have a high priest who is unable to sympathize with our weaknesses, but one who has similarly been tested in every way, yet without sin" (Hebrews 4:15).

Indeed, one cannot truly love until they, like Jesus, experience the crosses that come with it. In order to prove love, we are required to humble ourselves in the midst of suffering — the greater the pain, the purer the love.

In *Rosarium Virgins Marie*, St. Pope John Paul II describes the Sorrowful mysteries in the following way:

The Gospels give great prominence to the sorrowful mysteries of Christ. From the beginning Christian piety, especially during the Lenten devotion of the Way of the Cross, has focused on the individual moments of the Passion, realizing that here is found the culmination of the revelation of God's love and the source of our salvation. The Rosary selects certain moments from the Passion, inviting the faithful to contemplate them in their hearts and to relive them. The sequence of meditations begins with Gethsemane, where Christ experiences a moment of great anguish before the will of the Father, against which the weakness of the flesh would be tempted to rebel. There, Jesus encounters all the temptations and confronts all the sins of humanity, in order to say to the Father: "Not my will but yours be done" (Lk 22:42 and parallels). This "Yes" of Christ reverses the "No" of our first parents in the Garden of Eden. And the cost of this faithfulness to the Father's will is made clear in the following mysteries; by his scourging, his crowning with thorns, his carrying the Cross and his death on the Cross, the Lord is cast into the most abject suffering: Ecce homo!

This abject suffering reveals not only the love of God but also the meaning of man himself.

Ecce homo: the meaning, origin and fulfillment of man is to be found in Christ, the God who humbles himself out of love "even unto

death, death on a cross" (Phil 2:8). The sorrowful mysteries help the believer to relive the death
of Jesus, to stand at the foot of the Cross beside
Mary, to enter with her into the depths of God's
love for man and to experience all its life-giving
power.

(RVM, 22)

This week, as you contemplate the Sorrowful
Mysteries of the rosary, unite your personal sufferings to Christ on the cross. Doing so allows you to
escape the pains of this world and join them with
Christ crucified. As St. Catherine of Siena wrote, in
"lifting its feet from the affections of the earth, the
soul strips itself of vice." This is the first step toward
understanding the mystery of love.

Pray all of the Sorrowful Mysteries of the Rosary

Day 16

The Agony in the Garden

"I pray for them. I do not pray for the world but for the
ones you have given me, because they are yours."
- John 17:9

Throughout the Gospels, Jesus often disappears
from the scene in order to pray. He usually climbs a
mountain to avoid the attention of his followers and
spends entire nights in contemplative prayer. This
sacrifice of time and sleep were a normal part of his
life; it is almost as if he needed it to fill up his spiritual energy in order to complete his mission of
spreading the Good News.

The question is, what exactly *was* his prayer? In
the silence of the mountaintop, with which inexpressible groanings did the holy Spirit intercede
during his times of weakness? How did Jesus pray?
The Agony of the Garden gives us a glimpse of how
Jesus' prayers may have gone. Shortly after the Last
Supper, he brings his closest followers with him to

the garden where he asks them to keep watch while he prays alone. He didn't choose a mountaintop like before; for this prayer he remains on our level.

With the intensity of a death row inmate, Jesus pleads with the Father to attend to the weakness of his humanity. He, the second person of the Trinity, was able to submit to the terror that was his passion and death, but even God himself experienced the temptation of human weakness. He said, "My Father, if it is possible, let this cup pass from me; yet, not as I will, but as you will" (Matthew 26:39). If it were possible? Are not all things possible with God? Could not Jesus, true God and true man, have avoided the excruciating pain and suffering of the events to come and still have saved mankind from their sins?

Perhaps, but a life in union with God doesn't seek alternative options. There is no plan B with God, only plan A.

We are reluctant to become one with God. Like Jesus, we may be willing to submit to his will in order to achieve unity with him, but that doesn't make our fear disappear. We freeze. We hesitate. We doubt. And we rationalize our own will by discovering ways to "work around" God's will for us. We are human, after all, and the human condition will always provide us with a hesitation when our own will collides with God's.

That hesitation was experienced by God himself. In his prayer, he provided for our own courage to overcome it when he said, "They do not belong to the world any more than I belong to the world. Consecrate them in the truth. Your word is truth" (John 17:16-17).

While you are consecrating yourself to Jesus through Mary, you are echoing Jesus' words of consecration because he, the Word made flesh, has found within you his dwelling place. Through his agony in the garden, he sweat drops of blood that have purified your soul and prepared you for this total consecration to him. Along with Mary whose immaculate heart was made perfect through suffering, Jesus' sacred heart blazes with the heat of 10,000 suns so that yours may be made pure in the words of your promise.

His prayer thus went, "I have given them the glory you gave me, so that they may be one, as we are one, I in them and you in me, that they may be brought to perfection as one, that the world may know that you sent me, and that you loved them even as you loved me" (John 17:22-23).

Jesus' prayer was *your* consecration. Every word he spoke, every miracle he produced, every act he committed, and every prayer he made had one goal — to unite you with the Father in love. Like a bridegroom awaiting his beloved at the altar of sacrifice, he made his promise of consecration to you through the blood of his passion and death. Through your total consecration you join him in the garden in unity with the Father. Through this process you become one through the mystery of suffering.

"Now I rejoice in my sufferings for your sake, and in my flesh I am filling up what is lacking in the afflictions of Christ on behalf of his body, which is the church…"
- Colossians 1:24

Pray all of the Sorrowful Mysteries of the Rosary

Day 17

The Scourging at the Pillar

"Then Pilate took Jesus and had him scourged."

-John 19:1

We are nothing. We are weak, insignificant puffs of air when we look at the grand scheme of things. Take into account all of the people on the planet past, present, and future, all of the wonders of the natural world and the marvels of all that we cannot see and will never discover...

And yet, there's *you* amongst it all. A mere person going about life always trying to attain more. More money, more time, more exercise, more dessert.

We have a natural inclination to desire more because we see it as a means of achieving greatness. We strive for a promotion, more responsibilities, more titles and accolades because we desire from the depth of our being to be remembered, to be loved, to be noticed. We want to leave a legacy and, unfortunately, most of us go about it in the wrong way.

If we truly desire to leave a part of ourselves in this world, we must accept our weakness. We must realize our inconsequential existence and our extreme limitations before God. We must become weak so that we can become strong.

That's exactly what Jesus' entire ministry was about. First, he came down from heaven and became man, making himself like us in all things but sin. He fasted for forty days in the desert and was tempted by the devil. When he overcame that trial, he spent countless days and nights in an almost ceaseless barrage of activity — miracles, preaching, teaching, walking — all of this took its toll on his body and soul. But it didn't stop there. He was weakened spiritually during the Agony in the Garden. After that, he was weakened physically by the blows of whips from the Roman soldiers while he was cuffed to the pillar. He made no defense to their merciless lashes, but accepted them. Jesus became the weakest of all humans twice, once as a helpless baby in a manger and once again as he hung on the cross.

The Christian life is the truest paradox that one could ever dream up because we aspire for greatness, but we must do so through weakness, acquiring detachment from the world. Unfortunately, we tend to do the exact opposite — we become attached to worldly strength, stature, and perceived security. We spend countless hours working to better our careers, but we have no time to give to the poor. We spend more time on screens than with our loved ones, let alone the sick and the elderly. We eat finely crafted meals, but we find excuses to skip Mass and the Eucharist. We constantly seek the brief comforts of the world instead of the eternal comforts of God.

To be comfortable in a human body is the most difficult thing in the world to do. We desire to be strong, but we are not. We are weak, and if we can ignore the avarice that binds us to this world, we can discover the beaten and bruised God-man that binds us to the true power of His Father through our sufferings.

It is in our weakness that we are strong. It is in our service that we are made powerful. It is then that we realize that a rich person is not the one who has the most, but the one who needs the least.

Our Lady knew this well. In fact, all throughout the story of salvation it is the weak whom God calls to show his strength. David was a shepherd boy, but he defeated the giant Goliath and established Jerusalem as the Jewish religious center of the world. Joseph was a simple carpenter, but he led his wife and unborn son to Bethlehem where God was given to man. St. Francis, St. Paul, St. Dominic, St. Theresa of Calcutta, St. Terese of Lisieux, and countless others like them began as small seedlings in their faith, but blossomed into the fruit-bearing trees that now touch the heavens.

Today, and always, reflect upon the things that worry you, the pains, the struggles, the anxiety, and the sadness, and count them as the very things that give you true power.

"My brothers and sisters, count it pure joy when you are involved in every sort of trial. Realize that when your faith is tested this makes for endurance. Let endurance come to its perfection so that you may be fully mature and lacking in nothing."

- James 1:2-4

Pray all of the Sorrowful Mysteries of the Rosary

Day 18

The Crowning of Thorns

"They stripped off his clothes and threw a scarlet military cloak about him. Weaving a crown out of thorns, they placed it on his head, and a reed in his right hand. And kneeling before him, they mocked him, saying, 'Hail, King of the Jews!'"

-Matthew 27:28-29

Jesus was finally recognized as King, but it wasn't the coronation ceremony that we are familiar with — it was a crude, despicable display. The soldiers mocked him, spit upon him, and punched him in the face mercilessly. On top of that, they wove for him a crown of thorns and placed it upon his head and threw a scarlet cloak about him, mocking him and disrespecting his true Kingship.

And Jesus would have it no other way.

Jesus came to save sinners. The very men who insulted Jesus and robbed him of his dignity were the ones whom Jesus came to save. When Adam and

Eve fell, the perfection of the earth became hopelessly imperfect. The Prophet Isaiah foretold this mystical kingship between the perfect God and his imperfect land when he said, "Upon the land of my people shall come up thorns and briers" (32:13). Still later, Hosea prophesied that, "The thorn and the thistle shall come up on their altars" (10:8). Here, in the mystery of the Crowning of Thorns, we have the thorn and thistle descending upon the true Altar, Jesus Christ, who bears the weight of its intense pain for the purpose of uniting his people in sacrificial love.

Interestingly enough, the two symbols hoisted upon Jesus at this time, the crown of thorns and the scarlet cloak, are unifying in themselves in a unique way. Before the invention of the needle, seamsters and seamstresses would use different artifacts from their environment to sew hides and cloth together to make clothes. In hunting communities, bone was used to fuse two animal skins together. In other communities, thorns and needles were used. For example, the Aztec people who lived in present-day Mexico would use the needles of the maguey

(Agave) plant to string together the smashed pulp from the same plant in order to make their clothes. It was from this method of creating clothes that the tilma of St. Juan Diego was created which, to this day, still bears the miraculous image of Our Lady of Guadalupe.

The thorns placed upon Jesus' head are unitive because through them, the very fabric of man's soul was united to Christ' soul by the needle of suffering. Jesus, like the maguey plant, was beaten to a pulp so that the story of salvation could be woven into a flawless tapestry of divine making.

The cloak was also a unitive symbol. It, unlike the maguey plant, was a seamless piece of cloth and of great value to the Romans. Later on, when Jesus was hanging on the cross, the soldiers would cast lots to see who would get this cloak because they didn't dare split it into pieces due to its value. Since it was a pure cloak without seams, it represents God's perfection and unity, one that not even human beings dare to attempt to destroy.

Through these two items, Jesus achieves perfect suffering. The cloak represents God's perfection and the thorns represent the pain through which Our Lord would join his essence with our souls. The Crowning of Thorns is the divine seamster's tale of the true Emperor's new clothes — the crown of salvation and the robes of humility.

As you reflect on the Sorrowful Mysteries today, ask God to grant you the wisdom to recognize Christ in your sufferings. Then, and only then, will you discover their divine purpose.

"…that I might not become too elated, a thorn in the flesh was given to me, an angel of Satan, to beat me, to keep me from being too elated. Three times I begged the Lord about this, that it might leave me, but he said to me, 'My grace is sufficient for you, for power is made perfect in weakness'."

- 2 Corinthians 12:7-9

Pray all of the Sorrowful Mysteries of the Rosary

Day 19

The Carrying of the Cross

"A large crowd of people followed Jesus, including many women who mourned and lamented him."

-Luke 23:27

The Stations of the Cross are a Catholic tradition that give us insight into Jesus' journey from jail to Golgotha, the place he would be crucified. It begins with his condemnation and follows Jesus on the painstaking path to his death. At every step, the Stations illuminate the intense suffering and anguish that the weight of the cross had upon him and those who watched him persevere in silence.

After being condemned to death, he received the cross beam, walked, then fell to the ground with the pressure of the wood upon his already weakened body. There, Jesus met his mother's gaze. Their eyes meet in perfect silence. Heaven and earth are united in their weakness, his to hold up the cross and hers being unable to do anything to relieve his suffering.

Mary, the Mother of God, in her sinless grace cannot change the situation no matter how great the desire to plead that the Father have mercy upon his Son. Jesus could change the circumstances, but he is not willing to. In their silent stare, the two greatest characters in the story of salvation find strength in their unity and reason to persevere.

Mary was familiar with what I like to call "holy confusion," or not understanding the will of God, yet depending upon him regardless. She experienced such confusion on multiple occasions. When the Angel Gabriel announced to her that she would become the Mother of God, she said, "How can this be for I know no man?" (Luke 1:34). When the shepherds came to worship the child in the stable, Mary "pondered their words in her heart" (Luke 2:19). When they found Jesus in the Temple of Jerusalem, she and Joseph were astonished at his actions and she again "kept all these things in her heart" (Luke 2:51). And now, the words of the prophet Simeon came to crystal clarity, "Behold, this child is destined for the fall and rise of many in Israel, and to be a sign that will be contradicted (and you yourself a sword will pierce) so that the thoughts of many hearts may be revealed" (Luke 2:34-35).

Mary loved her son more than anyone else both before and after his life, death, and resurrection. She of all people would have the capability of seeing her only Son suffer the torment of this moment and to accept it. She shares in her son's passion and echoes within her soul the words of the prophet Isaiah, "He was oppressed, and he was afflicted, yet he opened not his mouth; he was like a lamb that is led to slaughter" (Isaiah 54:7).

It is in the silence of our hearts that we also join our sufferings with Mary and Jesus when we carry our own crosses through life. Jesus told his disciples, "If anyone wishes to come after me, he must deny himself and take up his cross daily and follow me" (Luke 2:23). Our crosses are nothing compared to the sufferings of Our Lord and Our Lady, but we must nevertheless accept their value to our souls. It is our responsibility to bear our misfortunes, vices, temptations, and sufferings with the same silent fervor as Christ. We must echo the words of Job, "We accept good things from God; should we not accept evil?" (Job 2:10).

Jesus and Mary knew that there are some circumstances through which God's will is made known through suffering. Fortunately for them, and for us, the two shared a bond of love that overshadowed their doubts and worries. Even at the point of intense suffering and imminent death, they made no effort to alter God's will. With every ounce of their being, their souls surely wanted nothing more than to return to the days of old back when Jesus sat upon his mother's lap and she held him with the tender caresses that only a mother can give her child.

Now, she'd hold him in her heart.

In this mystery of the Carrying of the Cross, she teaches us how to do the same.

"We adore you, O Christ, and we praise you. Because by your holy cross You have redeemed the world."

- Prayer from the *Stations of the Cross*

Pray all of the Sorrowful Mysteries of the Rosary

Day 20

The Crucifixion

"When they came to the place called the Skull,
they crucified him..."

-Luke 23:33

Death comes for us all. That fact remains in the back of our minds for the duration of our lives, and rightfully so. It provides us with a time limit to achieve the completion of our mission on earth. We know not when it will happen, nor how, but we do know that it is, indeed, coming.

Most of us worry about death. Like an ominous shadow it lurks, causing us to experience worry, anxiety, and pain. Indeed, death has a great power over us because it makes us human. It regulates our ambitions and harnesses our hopes. For those who are not truly living, death is a burden whose mantra reminds us, "You are running out of time."

However, death is also a catalyst toward good. Its presence provides us with a foundation for our sanity. In death, we realize that we are not to live forever in this life, that the legacy that we leave can have considerable effects on the world. In the words of Marcus Aurelius in the movie Gladiator, "What we do now echoes into eternity."

One could argue, then, that the best part about life is the death that motivates it. As Christians, we are given the charge to die to ourselves daily so as to rise up to Christ and make the ascent into the divine. There, we contemplate the true meaning of our lives and receive from God the means to accomplish the mission he has set before us to complete. Typically, this mission involves sacrifice, something that forces us to delve deep into the mystery of love for our brothers and sisters as we recognize Jesus within them, especially those most in need.

But, he doesn't want us to do it alone; he hasn't left that open for us: "When Jesus saw his mother and the disciple there whom he loved, he said to his mother, 'Woman, behold, your son.' Then he said to the disciple, 'Behold, your mother.' And from that hour the disciple took her into his home" (John 19:26-27).

At the very end of his life, Jesus gave to his mother to his most beloved disciple, a mystical gift that he gives to us all. She, the ideal woman, who was woven before the world began to be perfect, a model for all humanity to imitate, was destined to be our companion on the road to salvation. She, the "mother of all Christians" (Revelation 12:17), who raised the God-man to achieve his most perfect sacrifice of death on a cross, is to lead us to our own deaths of servitude so that we, too, can be crucified with Christ so that it is no longer we who live, but Christ within us (Galatians 2:20).

It is only in death that we meet Jesus and become him. It is only in death that we come to know him as he truly is through the relationship we have with Our Lady: "He comforts us in all our afflictions and thus enables us to comfort those who are in trouble, with the same consolation we have received from him. As we have shared much in the suffering of Christ, so through Christ do we share abundantly in his consolation" (2 Corinthians 1:3-4).

Who is this consolation? She is Our Lady. She shared most in the sufferings of Christ as only his mother could, and so through Christ, we share abundantly in her. For it us through her that all of God's graces flow. Pope Leo XII, in his *Iucunda semper*, wrote:

> ... when He [the Father] has been invoked with excellent prayers, our humble voice turns to Mary; in accordance with no other law than that law of conciliation and petition which was expressed as follows by St. Bernardine of Siena: 'Every grace that is communicated to this world has a threefold course. For by excellent order, it is dispensed from God to Christ, from Christ to the Virgin, from the Virgin to us.'

This is why total consecration to Jesus must occur through Mary. She is the unique middle ground that unites heaven and earth with her constant and consistent motherhood. She births us into life eternal (John 3:3, Revelation 12:17), she consoles us in our need (2 Corinthians 1:3-4), and she challenges us at every moment to "do whatever he tells [us]" (John 2:5).

Death, then, has no power over us when looked upon by the eyes of Our Lady and Our Lord, who received the most difficult blow at the cross. These two took the hit, and with perfect obedience to their mission, they defeated it through Christ's resurrection. The cross teaches us, then, that we can do the same thing if we learn from these two who remain with us on this side of life and on the other side of death, teaching us how to "work out our own salvation" (Philippians 2:12-13).

"... in suffering with Him as He died on the cross, she cooperated in the work of the Savior, in an altogether singular way, by obedience, faith, hope, and burning love, to restore supernatural life to souls. As a result she is our Mother in the order of grace."

- *Lumen gentium,* 61-62

Pray all of the Sorrowful Mysteries of the Rosary

Day 21

Mary's Perpetual Virginity

Many times you will hear people confused about the dogma of Mary's perpetual virginity. They'll argue that since sex is a positive thing that leads to procreation and marital bonding that it should follow that Mary was at liberty to lose her virginity to Joseph considering the Jewish laws of betrothal. It would also be fine, then, if she were to conceive other children so long as it was after she had conceived Jesus as a virgin.

The problem with this argument is that it misrepresents not only who Mary is, but more importantly who *Jesus* is. All Marian dogmas have as a rule the divine humanity of Jesus as its fulcrum. Mary's Perpetual Virginity is no different.

According to the Council of the Lateran in 649 A.D., Mary conceived "without any detriment to her virginity, which remained inviolate even after his birth."

The Catholic Church holds as dogma that Mary was a virgin before, during, and after Christ's conception. She remained a virgin for the sole purpose of honoring the novelty of her Son's divine Incarnation. To do so, she completed the equally novel act of remaining totally chaste so as to fulfill her mission as Mother to her Son (and to us, her spiritual children) to perfection.

The Catechism of the Catholic Church states,

From the first formulations of her faith, the Church has confessed that Jesus was conceived solely by the power of the Holy Spirit in the womb of the Virgin Mary, affirming also the corporeal aspect of this event: Jesus was conceived 'by the Holy Spirit without human seed.' The Fathers see in the virginal conception the sign that it truly was the Son of God who came in a humanity like our own. Thus St. Ignatius of Antioch at the beginning of the second century says:

'You are firmly convinced about our Lord, who is truly of the race of David according to the flesh, Son of God according to the will and power of God, truly born of a virgin,. . . he was truly nailed to a tree for us in his flesh under Pontius Pilate. . . he truly suffered, as he is also truly risen'. (*CCC*, 496)

The Catechism goes on to say,

Mary's virginity manifests God's absolute initiative in the Incarnation. Jesus has only God as Father. 'He was never estranged from the Father because of the human nature which he assumed. . . He is naturally Son of the Father as to his divinity and naturally son of his mother as to his humanity, but properly Son of the Father in both natures'. (*CCC*, 503)

In other words, the "absolute initiative" of God maintained that Mary would remain a Virgin forever so that Jesus would not be estranged from his heavenly Father *nor* his earthly mother. If Mary had

had children with Joseph, her time, attention, and mission would have been to them collectively and not to Jesus alone (and later to us, her spiritual children). This would have estranged her significantly from her call to remain loyal to her Son in every aspect of her being, including her sexuality.

The "absolute initiative" of God is present throughout the Bible in other contexts as well. For example, in the Old Testament we see the Ark of the Covenant as a type that precludes Mary's perpetual virginity. In Luke 1:39-45, Mary's cousin, Elizabeth, greets her with, "And why is this granted to me, that the mother of my Lord should come to me?" This refers back to 2 Samuel 6:9, in which the Old Testament type of Mary (the old Ark of the Covenant), was carried into the presence of King David who leapt for joy and said, "How can the ark of the Lord come to me?"

The Ark remained with David three months, and when it arrived, he danced. In a New Testament fulfillment of the type, Luke 1 records that Mary remained with Elizabeth for three months and John the Baptist leapt in Elizabeth's womb at the sound of Mary's greeting.

So, how does the Ark reflect Mary's perpetual virginity? According to the Old Testament, no one except the high priest could touch the Ark or even look inside of it, lest he die. If this was the case for the Old Testament type, which according to Hebrews 10:1 is no more than a shadow of the true New Testament fulfillment, then it would seem fitting that Mary would remain "untouched" by Joseph (or any other man for that matter) as well.

In today's culture, it is easy to rationalize a non-Virgin Mary because of our inclination to see marital sex as a positive, even holy act. After all, it was God who told us to multiply, right? The dogma of Mary's Perpetual Virginity stands as the lone example of how one perfect woman can honor the grace of the Incarnation through her chastity, thus glorifying Jesus all-the-more.

As we wrap up our week-long focus on the Sorrowful mysteries, we contemplate the mortifications of Christ's passion and death on the cross for the sake of our own purity in mind, body, and soul.

There is no better person to teach us how to be open to such grace than Our Lady who accompanied Him during his life in her perfect purity, as well as during his passion and death, the most perilous moment in the history of mankind.

Pray all of the Sorrowful Mysteries of the Rosary

Day 22

The Glorious Mysteries

The single greatest moment in the history of the world occurred that first Easter Sunday when Jesus rose from the dead. He defeated death itself and opened for us the gates to eternal life. We no longer were subjected to the eternal effects of our sins, but were freed from their shackles and given, for the first time, an eternal decision to make — to believe in Christ's promise of salvation through the forgiveness of our sins.

We as humans have a lifetime to make one, single, *eternal* decision — to believe that Christ died and rose from the dead to save us. Every other decision we make in this world is temporal: where to live, whom to marry, with which religious community to discern, and what to have for breakfast tomorrow morning are all decisions that pass when our earthly lives are over. The one decision that has everlasting consequences, however, remains embedded in the Glorious mysteries of the rosary, and it is our job to discover its enticing beauty before it is too late.

In *Rosarium Virgins Marie*, St. Pope John Paul II describes the Glorious mysteries in the following way:

> "'The contemplation of Christ's face cannot stop at the image of the Crucified One. He is the Risen One!' The Rosary has always expressed this knowledge born of faith and invited the believer to pass beyond the darkness of the Passion in order to gaze upon Christ's glory in the Resurrection and Ascension. Contemplating the Risen One, Christians rediscover the reasons for their own faith (cf. 1 Cor 15:14) and relive the joy not only of those to whom Christ appeared – the Apostles, Mary Magdalene and the disciples on the road to Emmaus – but also the joy of Mary, who must have had an equally intense experience of the new life of her glorified Son. In the Ascension, Christ was raised in glory to the right hand of the Father, while Mary herself

would be raised to that same glory in the Assumption, enjoying beforehand, by a unique privilege, the destiny reserved for all the just at the resurrection of the dead. Crowned in glory – as she appears in the last glorious mystery – Mary shines forth as Queen of the Angels and Saints, the anticipation and the supreme realization of the eschatological state of the Church.

At the centre of this unfolding sequence of the glory of the Son and the Mother, the Rosary sets before us the third glorious mystery, Pentecost, which reveals the face of the Church as a family gathered together with Mary, enlivened by the powerful outpouring of the Spirit and ready for the mission of evangelization. The contemplation of this scene, like that of the other glorious mysteries, ought to lead the faithful to an ever greater appreciation of their new life in Christ, lived in the heart of the Church, a life of which the scene of Pentecost itself is the great "icon". The glorious mysteries thus lead the faithful to greater hope for the eschatological goal towards which they journey as members of the pilgrim People of God in history. This can only impel them to bear courageous witness to that 'good news' which gives meaning to their entire existence.

(RVM, 23)

The story of salvation began in the Joyful Mysteries, continued into the Mysteries of Light, and seemingly culminated in the darkness of the Sorrowful Mysteries. But like all good stories, God saved the best chapter for last. As you contemplate the Glorious Mysteries this week, allow the God of our salvation to enter into your soul and enliven it with his glory.

Pray all of the Glorious Mysteries of the Rosary

Day 23

The Resurrection

"Why do you seek the living one among the dead?"

- Luke 24:5

Angels have a glorious sense of humor. When the disciples came to find Jesus after hearing of his resurrection, they ran as fast as they could to the tomb where angels greeted them with holy wit. They told them, "Why do you seek the living one among the dead?" One can only imagine the snicker they had to hold back at their statement.

And yet, their comment served as the key that unlocked the greatest realization the world has ever known. For they continued saying, "'He is not here, but he has been raised. Remember what he said to you while he was still in Galilee, that the Son of Man must be handed over to sinners and be crucified, and rise on the third day.' And they remembered his words."

They, the disciples who were told over and over again in several different ways during Jesus' ministry that he would die and rise to life again, finally "remembered his words."

How could they possibly forget?

Very easily.

We do it, too. How often do we receive the seed of faith with eager excitement to see it flourish, but then we realize that we have planted it upon the rocky ground where it cannot survive? Or perhaps it is planted amongst the thorns and then choked to death? How often do we act with zeal to attain the highest degree of knowledge and wisdom of our God and then succumb to the distractions of the world? Worse yet, how often do we justify our worldliness with "holy excuses" that rationalize our ignorance?

More often than we think.

And yet, the angels appear to us in their sly ways and remind us with their guiding words, "Why do you seek the living one among the dead?"

To their credit, the disciples who arrived at the empty tomb experienced an unbelievable truth that day. No one had ever raised himself from the dead without divine assistance (such as those whom the scriptures tell us Christ personally brought back), and no one has done so since. News like this was hard to fathom, and they needed a truly "holy excuse" to rationalize their ignorance. That is the power of sanctifying grace.

We who are human exist as an outpouring of God's love. Without him, we are nothing. This has always been the case, even before the resurrection. After the resurrection, however, we were given the immense blessing of sanctifying grace which operates in full force like a magnet to all of us who desire answers to our existential questions, meaning in our lives, and love in our hearts. When we run as fast as we can to this gift, we become like the disciples who ran to the tomb that Sunday morning, and we "remember his words."

St. Paul reminds us, "If we have died with Christ, we believe that we are also to live with him. We know that Christ, once raised from the dead, will never die again; death has no more power over him. His death was death to sin, once for all; his life is life

for God. In the same way, you must consider your-
selves dead to sin but alive for God in Christ Jesus"
(Romans 6:8-11).

Our Lady experienced sanctifying grace at the
moment of her conception. As a result, she was
given infused knowledge of divine truths, one of
which was the mystery of the resurrection. While
none of her knowledge was ever 100% complete (1
Corinthians 2:11), for no one can know the mind of
God, she of all people was the one who understood
his words the most due to her unique role as *Theotokos*, the God bearer and the Mother of God. This
was the reason she was able to persevere during the
passion and death of her Son. It was also the reason
that she maintained hope during the three days he
was in the tomb.

But, oh what joy she must have felt that Sunday
morning!

Her infused knowledge and unsurprising love is
what she shares with us as our spiritual mother. To
make your total consecration to her is to attain from
her the same graces that allowed her seed of faith to
be planted in rich soul so that it could "produce fruit

one hundred, or sixty, or thirty fold" (Matthew 13:8).

Mary *is* that rich soil in which we plant our seeds of hope. She is the same soil in which Our Lord was first sown and grown. And it is through her that all of us are born again and risen into life eternal.

"Blessed be the God and Father of our Lord Jesus Christ, who in his great mercy gave us a new birth to a living hope through the resurrection of Jesus Christ from the dead."

- 1 Peter 1:3

Pray all of the Glorious Mysteries of the Rosary

Day 24

The Ascension

"'...you will receive power when the holy Spirit comes upon you, and you will be my witnesses in Jerusalem, throughout Judea and Samaria, and to the ends of the earth.' When he had said this, as they were looking on, he was lifted up, and a cloud took him from their sight."

-Acts 1:8-9

As a lector, I always get excited for the Feast of the Ascension. Normally, the proclamation of Jesus' words are reserved for the priest or deacon whose privilege it is to read the Gospel. But, on the Feast of the Ascension, Jesus' words appear in the second reading which comes from the Acts of the Apostles, which means that a layman is able to read it even with the priest or deacon present. It is a tremendous honor not only to be able to read Jesus' words, but to lose oneself in the contemplation of this most mysterious event.

As the story unfolds, "While they [the disciples] were looking intently at the sky as he was going, suddenly two men dressed in white garments stood beside them. They said, 'Men of Galilee, why are you standing there looking at the sky? This Jesus who has been taken up from you into heaven will return in the same way as you have seen him going into heaven'" (Acts 1:10-11). One can only imagine the sense of loss, and even deception, that they felt at having lost Jesus yet again!

The first time, they lost him in death, which was logically fathomable because people die all the time. The second time, they lost him in his resurrected life, which was already mysterious in its own right; how much more perplexed they must have been to see him leave them again? We, too, would have wanted to remain there, staring at the sky, waiting for eternity for him to come back.

As it were, they returned to Jerusalem and "[a]ll these devoted themselves with one accord to prayer, together with some women, and Mary the mother of Jesus, and his brothers" (Acts 1:14). The disciples gathered with Mary to satiate their curiosity and sustain their hope in Christ. It was with her that they learned how to properly pray so as to make their own ascent to divine wisdom. It was with her that they, like Jesus, were given life.

Tinged with eternal wisdom and proper guidance, they forged within themselves the seeds of faith in Our Lady who nourished their growth with the water of her words, the soil of her presence, and the reflection of sunlight that was her Son. It was the Holy Spirit who would later bring the holy heat needed to solidify their souls as fully grown instruments of Christ's eternal mission.

The Ascension teaches us to maintain our faith during periods of obscurity. The disciples looked up into the sky as Jesus left them with the question "What gives?" on their minds. The only answer they were given was a promise that the Holy Spirit would eventually come to them, through the cloud that covered him from them.

In our spiritual lives, we often experience this same sensation that the disciples felt, that Jesus is too distant of a God to be properly understood. This

is actually true, for we were never meant to understand God completely. If we were able to do that, we
would *be* God. Jesus was hidden from them by a
cloud in the same way that the Blessed Sacrament is
hidden from us by the form of bread and wine; we
were never meant to see him clearly until the day we
meet him, face to face, during the beatific vision.

And so all of us, layman or woman, priest, religious, and unbelievers are surrounded daily by
clouds of doubt. We often ask ourselves, "What
gives?" The true question isn't *what* gives, but *Who*
gives. And the answer is Jesus, Who gives us his
Mother. She is the key to unlocking the mysteries of
Christ. She is the pure reflection of his light, and her
role is the same as it was on the day of the Ascension:
to teach, guide, and nourish us as we wait in joyful
anticipation for the holy Spirit to renew within us
the mystery of our faith.

"I will ask the Father, and he will give you another Ad-
vocate to be with you always, the Spirit of truth, which
the world cannot accept, because it neither sees nor

knows it. But you know it, because it remains with you, and will be in you."

- Jn. 14:16-17

Pray all of the Glorious Mysteries of the Rosary

Day 25

The Descent of the Holy Spirit

"When the time for Pentecost was fulfilled, they were all
in one place together. And suddenly there came from
the sky a noise like a strong driving wind, and it filled
the entire house in which they were. Then there appeared to them tongues as of fire, which parted and
came to rest on each one of them."

-Acts 2:1-3

Jesus' promise to send the Holy Spirit upon the
apostles came true in the Descent of the Holy Spirit,
otherwise known as Pentecost. Pentecost demon-
strates how the Church speaks the words of eternal
life through the Holy Spirit and with Mary. It represents the proper formula of evangelization beginning with God in whom truth has its essence, passing through Mary who gives truth a form in the person of Christ, to our Bishops who articulate truth in
every language so that it arrives to all people who
can then live truth and benefit from its saving grace.

What's more, Our Lady also teaches us the meaning of truth through her motherly guidance and contemplative openness in receiving the silent graces that overflow from God's everlasting love. She did this most effectively during the Descent of the Holy Spirit upon the apostles because she had already experienced the Holy Spirit's descent within her during the Incarnation. Who better to experience such a grace than with the Mother of God who gathered with them that day the Church was born? What's more, who better to teach the entire world of God's glory than she who had the entirety of God's glory within her?

Our Lady continues to teach all people across every culture the truth that is her Son, Jesus Christ. She has done this throughout the centuries in apparitions and locutions as a native of the cultures in the locations she has appeared. In Tenochtitlán, in present day Mexico, she appeared as an Aztec woman to St. Juan Diego and, through the image she left on his tilma, she converted millions of Indians and conquistadores to truth under the title of Our

Lady of Guadalupe. She spoke perfect Nahuatl, the tribal language of the Aztec people.

Our Lady of Fatima appeared to Sts. Francisco and Jacinta Marto, and their cousin Lucia and communicated with them in perfect Portuguese. She spoke to St. Bernadette Soubirous in perfect French under the title of the Immaculate Conception, but we commonly refer to her in this apparition as Our Lady of Lourdes. She even spoke to Sister Agnes Katsuko Sasagaw in Akita, Japan, who was completely deaf, in her native tongue.

Our Lady continues to reverberate the same linguistic and spiritual fervor of Pentecost through her constant intercession in our lives. While not all of us will experience an apparition or a locution, she is most easily contacted and moved with compassion for those who pray her rosary. How do we know? She has told us so.

According to her words to Alanus de Rupe, "All who recite the Rosary are my sons [and daughters, and brothers [and sisters] of my only son Jesus Christ." To add, she provides a unique promise that only a mother could make: "You shall obtain all you ask of me by the recitation of the Rosary."

For Our Lord and Our Lady, every day is a Pentecost for their children. Since they live outside of space and time, and we within them, the Holy Spirit is constantly being breathed upon us so that we can experience the evangelical power of his gifts of wisdom, understanding, counsel, fortitude, knowledge, piety, and fear of the Lord. In baptism, these gifts are given to us, in Confirmation they are made whole, and it is our Lady's desire to see them manifested in our lives during every moment of our existence.

This is why she comes down to us in apparitions. This is why she unites herself to us through the Rosary. This is why she guides us under the official title of Mary, Mother of the Church, enabling every person of every culture to do exactly what the apostles did on that first Pentecost: to proclaim the truth that leads to perfect clarity and true joy.

"Jesus said to them again, 'Peace be with you. As the Father has sent me, so I send you.' And when he had said this, he breathed on them and said to them, 'Receive the holy Spirit'."

- Jn 20:20-21

Pray all of the Glorious Mysteries of the Rosary

Day 26

The Assumption of the Blessed Virgin Mary

"The Immaculate Mother of God, the ever Virgin Mary, having completed the course of her earthly life, was assumed body and soul into heavenly glory."

-Pius XII, *Munificentissimus Deus,* 44

The Ark of the Covenant was the centerpiece of the Jewish faith in the Old Testament. It held within its walls the tablets in which God had written the Ten Commandments, Aaron's staff, and a piece of manna that had fallen from heaven. Most importantly, it was where the oracle, or the voice of God, resided, to which Moses and other leaders would often visit for guidance from God himself (Exodus 25:22).

Our Lady has commonly been compared to the Ark of the Covenant, hailed as the human Ark of the New Covenant, the holy womb in which the Messiah would make his dwelling and become man. While she played a pivotal role in carrying Our Lord within her, she was never to be considered his equal in holiness, but that's where the comparison to the Ark is most prevalent — she was the personification of a lifeless box to whom men would come and consult for ages. She was not God, nor did she have the wisdom that only he has, but she formed a mystical, incomparable union with him.

Because of this unique union, Mary was given the grace of passing from this world into eternal life without judgment.

This occurred for good reason, for God created his own mother. If you were God and you had the ability to create your own mother, wouldn't you create her just as perfect as you could? Being God, there is no greater form of excellence, no better mold to create than from the one in which Our Lord created Our Lady. This mold was so perfect that it provided her a pathway toward heaven without obstacles, without detours, without purgation.

This is why the Assumption of the Virgin makes logical sense. While there is no scientific proof to explain her entry into heaven in full body and soul, there are philosophical proofs that lead us to believe it.

First, she was sinless and thus would not necessarily need to suffer the consequence of original sin, which is death. Granted, Jesus didn't require this either, and he most certainly died, which is why many people believe that Mary did actually die physically before being assumed into heaven.

Second, she was God's mother and most loyal servant, thus meriting for her the first-fruits of sanctity and preference of entry into her Son's heavenly home.

Finally, she is represented in the book of Revelation (chapter 12) as the Mother of all Christians, thus already in heaven in body and soul and interceding for us constantly.

For these reasons, especially due to her intercession, we can easily *assume* that Mary is in heaven.

This intercession is freely given to us as the most perfect means through which we can attain our salvation. As St. Louis de Montfort writes, "She is the safest, easiest, shortest and most perfect way of approaching Jesus and will surrender themselves to her, body and soul, without reserve in order to belong entirely to Jesus" (*True Devotion*, p. 55). She places us in her Ark and sows the seeds of faith within us as we grow in piety and holiness. The end goal is to achieve the same glory as she did, to be united with God in heaven.

Mary's life was a continual experience of heaven on earth. She was united to God in mind, body, and soul to the highest degree and for that reason, God gave her the gift of returning to him in the Assumption.

This connection between heaven and earth is our relationship with Mary. She unites us in her rosary and binds us to her Son through our constant meditation on the virtues and promises that are contained in each mystery. It is the rope that we climb through the interior life that leads to the divine, the leash that keeps us safe from the temptations of the world.

My hope for you as you make this total consecration to Jesus through Mary is that, at the end of your life, you will have already experienced much of heaven before you are granted official access to its innermost dwellings. May your transition from this life into the next be like Mary's who surely knew the pearly gates before ever having passed through them.

"Arise, O Lord, into your resting place: you and the ark, which you have sanctified."

- Psalm 131:8

Pray all of the Glorious Mysteries of the Rosary

Day 27

The Coronation of Mary
as Queen of Heaven and Earth

"He has cast down the mighty from their thrones,
and has lifted up the lowly."

-Luke 1:52

There is no denying that Jesus Christ is Our Lord and King. As celebrated on the final Sunday of ordinary time, we commemorate his Kingship on the feast of Christ the King, honoring him as the ruler of the entire universe.

But, if Christ is our King, then who is our Queen?

Dr. Scott Hahn sheds some light on why the Catholic Church views Mary as the one who rightfully occupies this holy office:

In the ancient Near East, most nations were monarchies ruled by a king. In addition, most cultures practiced polygamy; so a given king often had several wives. This posed problems. First, whom should the people honor as queen? But more important, whose son should receive the right of succession to the throne? In most Near Eastern cultures, these twin problems were resolved by a single custom. The woman ordinarily honored as queen was not the wife of the king, but the mother of the king. (*Hail, Holy Queen,* p. 78)

And so, in ancient times, especially in the Davidic monarchy, the King's power rested in the hands of his mother. We see this in the person of Bathsheba, wife of King David and mother of King Solomon. While David was alive, she would prostrate herself before him as he welded more power than she (see 1 Kings 1:11-16, 22). However, after his death, we find the new king, King Solomon, bowing before her! (see 1 Kings 2:13-23) She, being the Queen mother, had received an increase in power by simply being the mother of the King.

Mary, then, is the Queen Mother in the Kingdom of Heaven and Earth due to the simple fact that she is the Mother of God. It was at the moment of the Annunciation that she rightfully became the queen of all of us. As St. John Damascene wrote: "When she became mother of the creator, she truly became queen of every creature."

One of the duties of the Queen Mother in Davidic times was to make requests to the King on behalf of those less powerful. Again, Bathsheba gives us another glimpse into such a request in the book of 1st Kings. It reads:

Bathsheba went to King Solomon, to speak to him on behalf of Adonijah. And the king rose to meet her, and bowed down to her; then he sat on his throne and had a seat brought for the king's mother; and she sat on his right. Then she said, 'I have one small request to make of you; do not refuse me.' And the king said to her, 'Make your request, my mother; for I will not refuse you.' (1 Kings 2:19-20)

If Solomon in all of his wisdom could grant the simple requests of Adonijah through the intercession of Bathsheba, how much more precious in the eyes of God are our requests when brought forth to him by Our Lady? Indeed, they become even more important, more valuable when they pass through her heavenly hands. For in her all of our merits, intentions, and desires are made pure. Like a mountain's pressure turning coal to diamonds, so does Our Lady take all that we ask and present it to her Son.

As you enter into your final days of preparation for total consecration to Jesus through Mary, know that the totality of our being will belong solely to Our Lady. She, the Queen mother, to whom we give the summation of our merits, does what she pleases with them in perfect union with God's will. Such a level of mysticism is impossibly out of reach for us with less power, less grace, and less piety, but in giving all that we are to Our Lady, we become more powerful in our humility, filled with more grace in our faith, and more pious in recognizing our inferiority to God's awesome power.

Thus says the Lord:
The heavens are my throne,
and the earth is my footstool.
What kind of house can you build for me;
what is to be my resting place?
My hand made all these things
when all of them came to be, says the Lord.
This is the one whom I approve:
the lowly and afflicted man who trembles at my
    word.

- Isaiah 66:1-2

Do not be afraid to give yourself completely to Our Lord through Mary. The greatest Saints to ever walk this earth, including Jesus himself, did so with the unyielding honor that was deserving of her Queenship. In her, you are given a clear pathway to God and an unwavering guide to show you the way.

Remember, O most gracious Virgin Mary,
    that never was it known that anyone who fled to
        your protection,
    implored your help or sought your intercession,

was left unaided.

Inspired with this confidence,

I fly to you, O Virgin of virgins, my Mother;

to you do I come, before you I stand, sinful and
sorrowful.

O Mother of the Word Incarnate,

despise not my petitions,

but in your mercy hear and answer me.

Pray all of the Glorious Mysteries of the Rosary

Day 28

The Assumption

We have come to an interesting moment in our journey toward understanding Mary's role in the salvation of souls. Not only have we delved deeply into each mystery of her most holy rosary, but we've also studied three of the four Marian dogmas that the Catholic Church has declared true. They are the declarations that she is recognized as the Mother of God, her Perpetual Virginity, and her Immaculate Conception. Today, we recognize the final Marian dogma that was divinely revealed to the Church and which, consequently, was illustrated in the fourth glorious mystery — her Assumption into heaven.

On November 1, 1950, Pope Pius XII declared in his Encyclical *Munificentissimus Deus*, "from the universal agreement of the Church's ordinary teaching authority we have a certain and firm proof, demonstrating that the Blessed Virgin Mary's bodily Assumption into heaven — which surely no faculty of the human mind could know by its own natural powers, as far as the heavenly glorification of the virginal body of the loving Mother of God is concerned — is a truth that has been revealed by God and consequently something that must be firmly and faithfully believed by all children of the Church" (*MD*, 12).

The Assumption had been debated for centuries by philosophers and theologians from all over the world. Since it was already divinely revealed through the Glorious mysteries of the rosary for centuries, the Catholic faithful had pondered the depths of this mystery for ages prior to its official declaration in the 20th century.

The crux of the Assumption is found in Mary's unabashed obedience to God throughout her lifetime as intertwined with her sinlessness. This most beautiful of God's creations was spotless and was thus freed from the requirement of death in the spiritual sense. Given her role as mother of God and Mother of the Church, she successfully "crushed the serpent's head with her heel" and, like her Son, defeated death. Her body and soul was thus carried up to heaven at the end of her earthly life and given the grace of overseeing the spiritual safety of all of her children who strive to achieve the goal of our faith — heaven.

The assumption may be seen as a consequence of Divine Motherhood. Being through, with, and for her Son on earth, it would seem fitting for Mary to be through, with, and for her Son in heaven, too. She was the generous associate of her Son on earth. The Assumption tells us that this association continues in heaven. Mary is indissolubly linked to her Son on earth and in heaven.

The Catechism of the Catholic Church states,

"Finally the Immaculate Virgin, preserved free from all stain of original sin, when the course of her earthly life was finished, was taken up body and soul into heavenly glory, and exalted by the Lord as Queen over all things, so that she might be the more fully conformed to her Son, the Lord of lords and conqueror of sin and death." The Assumption of the Blessed Virgin is a singular participation in her Son's Resurrection and an anticipation of the resurrection of other Christians:

> In giving birth you kept your virginity; in your Dormition you did not leave the world, O Mother of God, but were joined to the source of Life. You conceived the living God and, by your prayers, will deliver our souls from death. (*CCC*, 966)

In heaven, Mary's active involvement in salvation history continues. In *Lumen Gentium*, the teaching authority of the Church states, "Taken up to heaven, she did not lay aside her salvific duty ... By her maternal charity, she cares for the brethren of her Son, who still journey on earth surrounded by dangers and cultics, until they are led into the happiness of their true home" (§ 62). Mary is the "eschatological icon of the Church" (*CCC*, 972), meaning the Church contemplates in Mary her own end of times.

Mary's Immaculate Conception reveals the dignity of man and God's original (sinless) plan for him. Mary's Assumption is the complement to the Immaculate Conception in that it reveals mankind's ultimate destiny: a sharing, in both body and soul, in the very life and glory of God. The Assumption of Mary gives us a glimpse of the glory that is yet to be fully revealed; it is a source of hope for Christians.

Today, as we finish our week-long focus on the Glorious mysteries, let us contemplate the Assumption of Our Lady and provide her our confidence that she will one day guide us along a similar pathway to heaven. For it is to her that we pray, "Holy Mary, Mother of God, pray for us sinners, now *and at the hour of our death.*"

Pray all of the Glorious Mysteries of the Rosary

The Three-Day Purge

Day 29

The First Day of Purging

There comes a moment in every Saint's spirituality in which they undergo the process of total transformation to the will of God. St. Paul tells us, "Whoever is in Christ is a new creation: the old things have passed away; behold, new things have come" (2 Corinthians 5:17). Becoming a new creation, however, doesn't happen overnight. Moses spent forty years in exile in Mid'i·an as he prepared to free the Jews from Egypt, and St. Paul spent three days in Damascus without food or drink nor his eyesight as he underwent the process of conversion. Jesus spent forty days in the desert while being tempted by the devil prior to beginning his own ministry. It seems, then, that the first step in being able to understand and accept God's will for our lives is to take a step back from our current realities and to purge ourselves from some of the things that bring us comfort and security.

Relinquishing some of the things that maintain our lives is an effective means of allowing God to take total control of us. In our detachment to things, we are more able to depend totally on God's grace so as to submit ourselves to his will more perfectly. This is why the Church joins together to purge itself of the distractions of the world during the weeks leading up to Easter and Christmas. Lent and Advent provide us with the proper means of preparation through which we are able to accept the intense graces that are poured out during the weeks in which we celebrate Christmas and Easter.

During this part of the process of total consecration to Jesus through Mary, it seems fitting, then, that we should also prepare ourselves through detachment. We do this to imitate Our Lord and empty ourselves, taking the form of a slave (Philippians 2:7) so that our hearts and minds will be fixated upon the holiness that is beyond us, impossible to reach through our own efforts. It is only through Our Lady that we can be transformed into the fullness of our potential. To come to her in humbleness is to come to her like Christ did.

Interestingly enough, in her very name, Mary, we come to discover the means through which we can accomplish this detachment.

The "M" stands for Mortification, also known as fasting. It is common for the Saints to undergo the long and tiresome task of fasting during their transformation into holier people. Jesus did it often and told his disciples that there were certain demons that could not be cast out unless they had fasted a great deal (Matthew 17:21). Fasting is a necessary component to total consecration as it weakens our bodies so as to strengthen our will toward the things of God.

For the next three days, consider how you would like to fast. Perhaps you will skip a meal each day, or give up a daily snack or drink that you frequently crave. At the very least, take on the Friday fasting rules that you observe during Lent in your region of the world.

The "A" in Mary's name stands for Adoration. St. James tells us to humble ourselves before the Lord and he will lift us up (James 4:10). Spending time before our Lord in the Blessed Sacrament provides a mountain of grace to the one who comes to him with a quiet disposition. If your diocese has a perpetual adoration chapel, find a way to get there once a day for the next three days. If this is not an option, ask your parish priest to provide you access to the adoration chapel for silent prayer. Even if the Blessed Sacrament isn't exposed, you receive the same graces when you pray before the tabernacle. The key is proximity for those who are able to achieve it.

If neither of these options is possible, then schedule a time during your day to be alone with the Lord in silent prayer.

The "R" stands for retreat. It is likely very impractical that you have the ability to leave home to attend a retreat center in your area or even to camp outside in a remote place. If you can do that, great, but most of us simply can't leave for three days due to our multiple responsibilities. To those people the word "retreat" refers to the detachments that you can make to better center yourself on listening to the voice of God. Through fasting and adoration, you've disposed yourself to many graces, but in detaching yourself from the things of the world in your daily life, you maximize the possibility of allowing more grace into your soul. By turning off your television, not accessing social media, washing your dishes by hand, not listening to music, etc., you create for yourself a remote place in which you can properly contemplate in silence the divine at every moment.

The "Y" stands for yearning. As St. Paul teaches us, "In the same way, the Spirit too comes to the aid of our weakness; for we do not know how to pray as we ought, but the Spirit itself intercedes with inexpressible groanings. And the one who searches hearts knows what is the intention of the Spirit, because it intercedes for the holy ones according to God's will" (Romans 8:26-27). These inexpressible groanings are our silent yearnings to become more holy, more acceptable to God than our current state. We long for the perfection of our souls, and we do everything in our power to come to the fulness of that potential, but as the verse above explains, the Spirit comes to the aid of our weakness. When we act upon our yearnings, the spirit completes them and overtakes us, much like he did with Our Lady during the Annunciation and the Apostles during Pentecost.

So, Mary's name is an acronym on how to prepare for God's grace.

(M)ortification
(A)doration
(R)etreat
(Y)earning

Let's pray that these next three days are enough to become her servants so that we can approach her son, Jesus, in total consecration to him.

Pray all of the Joyful Mysteries of the Rosary

Day 30

The Second Day of Purging

Our Lady is the Mother of all humanity. She is the unique, unitive force that joins heaven and earth and all that intertwines between both worlds. She is the Queen of Angels and the Star of the Sea, the Protectress of the Poor and the Seat of Wisdom. In her, all have a focal point to which we are magnetized by her beauty, virtue, and peace.

Unfortunately, the rest of humanity differs in their willingness to be attracted by not only her beauty, virtue, and peace, but *any* beauty, virtue, or peace. Not all, in fact not many, have risen to the heights of spirituality to meet her. Consequently, many have fallen into the trap of sin and temptation which blurs our vision and keeps us from attaining the spiritual clarity that only she can give. As a result, we have selective tunnel vision through which we see only what we want to see and not the reality of the world around us.

When that happens, or relationships are based
not on the love that binds us to one another, but on
the benefits we can receive from them. We see people for what they can offer us, not for what we can
offer them, and our society becomes weak because
of our own selfishness. Divorce rates climb, abor-
tion becomes commonplace, nations war against
nations, and the poor become poorer. Such is the
way of the world, sadly.

Whether you are the leader of the most powerful
nation in the world or you are a boy rummaging the
street for loose change, your relationships are what
provide you strength and love in this world. Our
Lady and Our Lord have sewn your seed, and they
have fostered your growth into who you are today.
They've given you the intelligence and talents to
overcome obstacles and rise up to your current state
of success and spiritual peace.

But it may be that not all of your relationships
are healthy. It may be that those whom God has sent
you to work with, live with, be with, and serve with
are not as closely connected to God's life-giving vine

as you would like. It is very possible that you might not be as connected as you would like either.

While the preparation for total consecration is considered an individual response to follow Our Lord and Our Lady to a more perfect degree, the truth is that we cannot do anything of spiritual worth alone. More often than not, the community that God desires for us is broken, or at least bent by the sins we commit toward one another. Jesus told us that if we have a grievance with our brother, we must leave our gift at the altar, make amends with our brother, and then return to make our offering (Matthew 5:23-24). In essence, then, we need the forgiveness not only of God to achieve the fulness of grace, but also the forgiveness of the ones we hurt and the ones who hurt us.

Today, fortify yourself in God by uniting your relationships to Our Lady. She, being the Queen of Angels, has a unique power in that she is able to enter into the most hard of hearts and make them open to the messages of her children. Since the word angel means "messenger," the first step toward reviving your broken relationships with those you have caused grievance through your sins, or with those who have sinned against you, is to pray to your guardian angel, their guardian angel, and Mary to help alleviate the pain that has caused your division.

If you are able, take action to bridge the divide between you. Give them a call. Send them a handwritten letter. Show up at their doorstep. Be the one who seeks peace in your relationship.

Our relationships create the Church. Our Lady leads us toward the mercy of God and the unmerited joy of forgiveness. Putting these into practice in our own lives is the hardest thing in the world to do. Our pride and security restrain us from establishing peace sometimes, and it is up to us to overcome this by thinking as God does, not as humans do (Matthew 16:23).

May this second day of purging be the beginning of your total consecration to others, especially your loved ones, because you cannot consecrate yourself to Our Lady unless you are ready to give yourself completely to those whom God has sent you to love.

Pray all of the Luminous Mysteries of the Rosary

Day 31

The Third Day of Purging

In a world of rampant consumerism and the "throw away" culture, I still believe that those who are economically stable have within themselves a lot more giving than they believe they are capable of. The fact is, most of us are simply comfortable giving of our surplus and leaving it at that. We give the $1 bill in our pocket to the homeless man begging on the corner, but we keep the $20 so we can pick up a burger and some fries on the way home. We did our good deed for the day, and we call it good. But when we take a bite of that burger, the taste of guilt consumes us. This is most definitely not good.

When the Saints become truly convinced of their mission, there is a common phrase that occurs in almost all of their biographies, "And then, they sold all that they had and gave the money to the poor." This heroic act of selfless dependence on God and detachment from things is a special calling, one that takes much goodwill on the part of the person who is giving it.

Not all of us are called to give to such a heroic degree. The husband and father of seven children has a different economic mindset when compared to the single, debt free, 25-year-old who is discerning entering religious life with the Brothers of St. Francis. Regardless of who you are and where you are in your ability to give to others, the Holy Spirit's gifts of prudence and right judgment regulate our potential for giving.

However, not all that can be given is related to economic stability nor the worth of physical products dispersed. Helping the poor takes more than a signed check — it takes an open heart. In the words of Saint Mother Teresa, "You must give until it hurts." (Speech at the National Prayer Breakfast, 1994)

Our Lord and Our Lady care for those who are most in need of God's mercy. The poor and destitute, the sick and suffering, the incarcerated and the lonely, the hungry and forlorn, the homeless, the children, the widow, the addict, all of these are those whom we are responsible for lifting up in not only our prayers, but also our actions and economic support.

On this, your third day of purging, consider how you can help those most in need of God's mercy on the three levels I just mentioned:

In prayer
In act
In economic support

Make a plan for the days and weeks after you complete your total consecration. Make charitable giving part of your budget and part of your weekly schedule. Block off time to strategize exactly how you plan on helping others given the time, talents, and treasures you have already been given by Our Lord.

Then, execute.

Pray all of the Sorrowful Mysteries of the Rosary

Day 32

Preparing Your Declaration of Consecration

Today is the eve of your total consecration. You have reflected on the mysteries of Our Lord and Our Lady through the recitation of the Rosary. You have purged yourself from your worldly attachments. You have become the spiritual catalyst for someone else through redemptive suffering. Finally, you've brainstormed a strategy to help the poor using your time, talents, and treasure.

With these preparations, you've come to the threshold of a more perfect union with God as prepared for you by the Blessed Virgin. Like a bride approaching the altar to become one with the bridegroom, so you come to the gates of heaven to join your soul with that of Our Lady who will make it most holy if you are willing to remain under the protection of her heavenly mantle.

Today, you will prepare your final consecration prayer. Like all unitive celebrations, the one being united must orally profess their desire to acknowledge with their will what God has placed within their hearts. They are drawn to make this profession using their own unique words, for no soul expresses itself the same way.

For that reason, it is important that you take the time to sit and reflect on all that Our Lord and Our Lady have done with your soul these past thirty-two days. It is equally important to respond to their work by producing an oral profession of faith that includes the following key aspects:

Total dependence on Our Lady

The giving of all merits to her

The promise of doing whatever she or God asks of you

The promise to actively serve God's people with pious zeal and holy fervor.

As you write the words you'll declare in your consecration, be sure to include those aspects on top of whatever other promises you will fulfill, requests for aid that you need, and words of praise that you see fit.

To give you an idea of what a final total consecration prayer looks like, here are two examples. The first is from arguably the most Marian man to have ever existed (save Jesus and Joseph), St. Louis de Montfort, original author of *Preparation for Total Consecration*, *True Devotion*, and *The Secret of the Rosary*. The second is from a greater sinner, yours truly.

St. Louis de Montfort's Total Consecration Prayer:

O Eternal and Incarnate Wisdom! O sweetest and most adorable Jesus! True God and True Man, only Son of the Eternal Father, and of Mary ever Virgin! I adore Thee profoundly in the bosom and glory of Thy Father during eternity; and I adore Thee also in the virginal bosom of Mary, Thy most worthy Mother, in the time of Thine Incarnation.

I give Thee thanks, that Thou hast annihilated Thyself taking the form of a slave, in order to rescue me from the cruel slavery of the devil. I praise and glorify Thee, that Thou hast been pleased to submit

Thyself to Mary, Thy holy Mother, in all things, in order to make me Thy faithful slave through her. But alas! Ungrateful and faithless as I have been, I have not kept the promises which I made so solemnly to Thee in my baptism; I have not fulfilled my obligations; I do not deserve to be called Thy child nor yet Thy slave; and as there is nothing in me which does not merit Thine anger and Thy repulse, I dare no more come by myself before Thy Most Holy and August Majesty. It is on this account that I have recourse to the Intercession of Thy most holy Mother, whom Thou hast given me for a Mediatrix with Thee. It is by her means that I hope to obtain of Thee contrition, and the pardon of my sins, the acquisition and the preservation of wisdom. I salute Thee, then, O Immaculate Mary living tabernacle of the Divinity, where the Eternal Wisdom willed to be hidden and to be adored by Angels and by men. I hail thee, O Queen of heaven and earth to whose empire everything is subject which is under God.

I salute Thee, O sure refuge of sinners, whose mercy fails no one. Hear the desires which I have of the Divine Wisdom; and for that end receive the vows and offerings which my lowness presents to thee.

I, [Name], a faithless sinner-I renew and ratify to-day in thy hands the vows of my Baptism; I renounce for ever Satan, his pomps and works; and I give myself entirely to Jesus Christ, the Incarnate Wisdom, to carry my cross after Him all the days of my life, and to be more faithful to Him than I have ever been before.

In the presence of all the heavenly court I choose thee this day for my Mother and Mistress. I deliver and consecrate to thee as Thy slave, my body and soul, my goods, both interior and exterior, and even the value of all my good actions, past present and future; leaving to you the entire and full right of disposing of me, and of all that belongs to me, without exception, according to Thy good pleasure to the greatest glory of God, in time and in eternity.

Receive O gracious Virgin, this little offering of my slavery, in honour of, and in union with, that subjection which the Eternal Wisdom deigned to have thy Maternity, in homage to the power which both of you have over this little worm and miserable sinner, and in thanksgiving for the privileges with which the Holy Trinity hath favoured thee. I protest, that I wish, henceforth, as thy true slave, to seek thy honour, and to obey thee in all things.

O admirable Mother, present me to thy Dear Son, as His eternal slave, so that as He hath redeemed me by thee, by thee He may receive me.

O Mother of mercy, get me the grace to obtain the true Wisdom of God, and for that end place me in the number of those whom thou lovest, whom thou teachest, whom thou leadest, and whom thou nourishest and protectest, as thy children and thy slaves. O Faithful Virgin, make me in all things so perfect a disciple, imitator and slave of the Incarnate Wisdom, Jesus Christ thy Son, that I may attain, by thy intercession and by thy example, to the fullness of His age on earth, and of His glory in heaven. Amen.

My Consecration Prayer (as prayed with my wife, Maribel)

We, Maribel and TJ Burdick, ask the Holy Spirit to dwell in us through our consecration to Jesus through Mary. We declare that all of our actions, gifts, joy, and sadness be for you a spiritual gift that will be dedicated through your unique and motherly intercession.

Guide our marriage along the glorious pathway that ends in the open arms of your Son in whom we find true union, true happiness, true love.

We ask that our children also become part of this consecration until they are called to partake in their own personal, unique consecrations to you.

We desire to be for you spiritual gifts that connect those most in need to your immaculate heart.

Our Lady of Guadalupe, Mystic Rose, Patroness of the Americas and Protectress of the unborn, we place ourselves in your hands so that you would bring our offerings to perfection for Jesus.

Your turn. After praying the Glorious Mysteries of the rosary, spend some time today writing your declaration of consecration. Let the spirit guide your pen.

Pray all of the Glorious Mysteries of the Rosary

Day 33

Total Consecration

Consecrating yourself to Jesus through Mary is like a marriage. You can go through a preparation in mind, body, and soul, but, truthfully, there is nothing that can fully prepare you for the reality that total consecration to another entails. In marriage, we promise our complete selves to our spouses until death do we part. In total consecration, we effectively bind ourselves to God in death to ourselves.

Much like celebrating the Sacrament of Matrimony, we know not what sacrifices we will need to make after our promise has been made. For better or for worse, in sickness and in health, in prosperity and poverty, we have no idea what our journey will bring. But, we will have someone to travel with, the supreme guide forged by God's own hand to be "full of grace" and "blessed among all woman." She is the handmaid of the Lord and our spiritual mother. It is through her that we can truthfully, and totally, belong to Jesus.

When Our Lady appeared to St. Juan Diego in present-day Mexico, she looked upon him and saw the worry in his heart. She gazed into the soul of her most humble servant and said, "Am I not here who am your Mother? Are you not under my shadow and protection? Am I not your fountain of life? Are you not in the folds of my mantle? In the crossing of my arms? Is there anything else you need?"

Today, you will make your final consecration to become one with Jesus through Mary. You know not where this relationship will take you. The only thing you do know is that from here on out your soul has been willfully given to the Mother of God to be used for whatever purpose her Immaculate Heart desires.

It just so happens that this purpose is also what Jesus' Sacred Heart desires. It is also what *your* heart *actually* desires. "Listen and let it penetrate your heart...do not be troubled or weighed down with grief. Do not fear any illness or vexation, anxiety or pain. ***Am I not here who am your Mother?***"

Pray all of the Glorious Mysteries of the Rosary

Appendix

How to pray the Rosary

This section comes from the papal document *Rosarium Virgins Marie* and has been provided for you verbatim for the purpose of introducing you to the Rosary as prescribed by the Magisterium of the Catholic Church.

Announcing each mystery

Announcing each mystery, and perhaps even using a suitable icon to portray it, is as it were to open up a scenario on which to focus our attention. The words direct the imagination and the mind towards a particular episode or moment in the life of Christ. In the Church's traditional spirituality, the veneration of icons and the many devotions appealing to the senses, as well as the method of prayer proposed by Saint Ignatius of Loyola in the Spiritual Exercises, make use of visual and imaginative elements (the compositio loci), judged to be of great help in concentrating the mind on the particular mystery. This is a methodology, moreover, which corresponds to the inner logic of the Incarnation: in Jesus, God wanted to take on human features. It is through his bodily reality that we are led into contact with the mystery of his divinity.

This need for concreteness finds further expression in the announcement of the various mysteries of the Rosary. Obviously these mysteries neither replace the Gospel nor exhaust its content. The Rosary, therefore, is no substitute for lectio divina; on the contrary, it presupposes and promotes it. Yet, even though the mysteries contemplated in the Rosary, even with the addition of the mysteria lucis, do no more than outline the fundamental elements of the life of Christ, they easily draw the mind to a more expansive reflection on the rest of the Gospel, especially when the Rosary is prayed in a setting of prolonged recollection.

Listening to the word of God

In order to supply a Biblical foundation and greater depth to our meditation, it is helpful to follow the announcement of the mystery with the proclamation of a related Biblical passage, long or short, depending on the circumstances. No other words can ever match the efficacy of the inspired word. As we listen, we are certain that this is the word of God, spoken for today and spoken "for me".

If received in this way, the word of God can become part of the Rosary's methodology of repetition without giving rise to the ennui derived from the simple recollection of something already well known. It is not a matter of recalling information but of allowing God to speak. In certain solemn communal celebrations, this word can be appropriately illustrated by a brief commentary.

Silence

Listening and meditation are nourished by silence. After the announcement of the mystery and the proclamation of the word, it is fitting to pause and focus one's attention for a suitable period of time on the mystery concerned, before moving into vocal prayer. A discovery of the importance of silence is one of the secrets of practicing contemplation and meditation. One drawback of a society dominated by technology and the mass media is the fact that silence becomes increasingly difficult to achieve. Just as moments of silence are recommended in the Liturgy, so, too, in the recitation of the Rosary it is fitting to pause briefly after listening to the word of God, while the mind focuses on the content of a particular mystery.

The "Our Father"

After listening to the word and focusing on the mystery, it is natural for the mind to be lifted up towards the Father. In each of his mysteries, Jesus always leads us to the Father, for as he rests in the Father's bosom (cf. Jn 1:18) he is continually turned towards him. He wants us to share in his intimacy with the Father, so that we can say with him: "Abba, Father" (Rom 8:15; Gal 4:6). By virtue of his relationship to the Father he makes us brothers and sisters of himself and of one another, communicating to us the Spirit which is both his and the Father's. Acting as a kind of foundation for the Christological and Marian meditation which unfolds in the repetition of the Hail Mary, the Our Father makes meditation upon the mystery, even when carried out in solitude, an ecclesial experience.

The ten "Hail Marys"

This is the most substantial element in the Rosary and also the one which makes it a Marian prayer par excellence. Yet when the Hail Mary is properly understood, we come to see clearly that its Marian character is not opposed to its Christological character, but that it actually emphasizes and increases it. The first part of the Hail Mary, drawn from the words spoken to Mary by the Angel Gabriel and by Saint Elizabeth, is a contemplation in adoration of the mystery accomplished in the Virgin of Nazareth. These words express, so to speak, the wonder of heaven and earth; they could be said to give us a glimpse of God's own wonderment as he contemplates his "masterpiece" – the Incarnation of the Son in the womb of the Virgin Mary. If we recall how, in the Book of Genesis, God "saw all that he had made" (Gen 1:31), we can find here an echo of that "pathos with which God, at the dawn of creation, looked upon the work of his hands." The repetition of the Hail Mary in the Rosary gives us a share in God's own wonder and pleasure: in jubilant amazement we acknowledge the greatest miracle of history. Mary's prophecy here finds its fulfillment: "Henceforth all generations will call me blessed" (Lk 1:48).

The centre of gravity in the Hail Mary, the hinge as it were which joins its two parts, is the name of Jesus. Sometimes, in hurried recitation, this centre of gravity can be overlooked, and with it the connection to the mystery of Christ being contemplated. Yet it is precisely the emphasis given to the name of Jesus and to his mystery that is the sign of a meaningful and fruitful recitation of the Rosary. Pope Paul VI drew attention, in his Apostolic Exhortation Marialis Cultus, to the custom in certain regions of highlighting the name of Christ by the addition of a clause referring to the mystery being contemplated.(37) This is a praiseworthy custom, especially during public recitation. It gives forceful expression to our faith in Christ, directed to the different moments of the Redeemer's life. It is at once a profession of faith and an aid in concentrating our meditation, since it facilitates the process of assimilation to the mystery of Christ inherent in the repetition of the Hail Mary. When we repeat the name of Jesus – the only name given to us by which we may hope for salvation (cf. Acts 4:12) – in close association with the name of his Blessed Mother, almost as if it were done at her suggestion, we set out on a path of assimilation meant to help us enter more deeply into the life of Christ.

From Mary's uniquely privileged relationship with Christ, which makes her the Mother of God, Theotókos, derives the forcefulness of the appeal we make to her in the second half of the prayer, as we entrust to her maternal intercession our lives and the hour of our death.

The "Gloria"

Trinitarian doxology is the goal of all Christian contemplation. For Christ is the way that leads us to the Father in the Spirit. If we travel this way to the end, we repeatedly encounter the mystery of the three divine Persons, to whom all praise, worship and thanksgiving are due. It is important that the Gloria, the high-point of contemplation, be given due prominence in the

Rosary. In public recitation it could be sung, as a way of giving proper emphasis to the essentially Trinitarian structure of all Christian prayer.

To the extent that meditation on the mystery is attentive and profound, and to the extent that it is enlivened – from one Hail Mary to another – by love for Christ and for Mary, the glorification of the Trinity at the end of each decade, far from being a perfunctory conclusion, takes on its proper contemplative tone, raising the mind as it were to the heights of heaven and enabling us in some way to relive the experience of Tabor, a foretaste of the contemplation yet to come: "It is good for us to be here!" (Lk 9:33).

The concluding short prayer

In current practice, the Trinitarian doxology is followed by a brief concluding prayer which varies according to local custom. Without in any way diminishing the value of such invocations, it is worthwhile to note that the contemplation of the mysteries could better express their full spiritual fruitfulness if an effort were made to conclude each mystery with a prayer for the fruits specific to that particular mystery. In this way, the Rosary would better express its connection with the Christian life. One fine liturgical prayer suggests as much, inviting us to pray that, by meditation on the mysteries of the Rosary, we may come to "imitate what they contain and obtain what they promise."

Such a final prayer could take on a legitimate variety of forms, as indeed it already does. In this way, the Rosary can be better adapted to different spiritual traditions and different Christian communities. It is to be hoped, then, that appropriate formulas will be widely circulated, after due pastoral discernment and possibly after experimental use in centres and shrines particularly devoted to the Rosary, so that the People of God may benefit from an abundance of authentic spiritual riches and find nourishment for their personal contemplation.

The Rosary beads

The traditional aid used for the recitation of the Rosary is the set of beads. At the most superficial level, the beads often become a simple counting mechanism to mark the succession of Hail Marys. Yet they can also take on a symbolism which can give added depth to contemplation.

Here the first thing to note is the way the beads converge upon the Crucifix, which both opens and closes the unfolding sequence of prayer. The life and prayer of believers is centred upon Christ. Everything begins from him, everything leads towards him, everything, through him, in the Holy Spirit, attains to the Father.

As a counting mechanism, marking the progress of the prayer, the beads evoke the unending path of contemplation and of Christian perfection. Blessed Bartolo Longo saw them also as a "chain" which links us to God. A chain, yes, but a sweet chain; for sweet indeed is the bond to God who is also our Father. A "filial" chain which puts us in tune with Mary, the "handmaid of the Lord" (Lk1:38) and, most of all, with Christ himself, who, though he was in the form of God, made himself a "servant" out of love for us (Phil 2:7).

A fine way to expand the symbolism of the beads is to let them remind us of our many relationships, of the bond of communion and fraternity which unites us all in Christ.

The opening and closing

At present, in different parts of the Church, there are many ways to introduce the Rosary. In some places, it is customary to begin with the opening words of Psalm 70: "O God, come to my aid; O Lord, make haste to help me", as if to nourish in those who are praying a humble awareness of their own insufficiency. In other places, the Rosary begins with the recitation of the Creed, as if to make the profession of faith the basis of the contemplative journey about to be undertaken. These and similar customs, to

the extent that they prepare the mind for contemplation, are all equally legitimate. The Rosary is then ended with a prayer for the intentions of the Pope, as if to expand the vision of
the one praying to embrace all the needs of the
Church. It is precisely in order to encourage this
ecclesial dimension of the Rosary that the
Church has seen fit to grant indulgences to those
who recite it with the required dispositions.

If prayed in this way, the Rosary truly becomes a spiritual itinerary in which Mary acts as
Mother, Teacher and Guide, sustaining the
faithful by her powerful intercession. Is it any
wonder, then, that the soul feels the need, after
saying this prayer and experiencing so profoundly the motherhood of Mary, to burst forth
in praise of the Blessed Virgin, either in that
splendid prayer the Salve Regina or in the Litany of Loreto? This is the crowning moment of
an inner journey which has brought the faithful
into living contact with the mystery of Christ
and his Blessed Mother.

Distribution over time

The Rosary can be recited in full every day, and there are those who most laudably do so. In this way it fills with prayer the days of many a contemplative, or keeps company with the sick and the elderly who have abundant time at their disposal. Yet it is clear – and this applies all the more if the new series of mysteria lucis is included – that many people will not be able to recite more than a part of the Rosary, according to a certain weekly pattern. This weekly distribution has the effect of giving the different days of the week a certain spiritual "colour", by analogy with the way in which the Liturgy colours the different seasons of the liturgical year.

According to current practice, Monday and Thursday are dedicated to the "joyful mysteries", Tuesday and Friday to the "sorrowful mysteries", and Wednesday, Saturday and Sunday to the "glorious mysteries". Where might the "mysteries of light" be inserted? If we consider that the "glorious mysteries" are said on both

Saturday and Sunday, and that Saturday has always had a special Marian flavour, the second
weekly meditation on the "joyful mysteries",
mysteries in which Mary's presence is especially
pronounced, could be moved to Saturday.
Thursday would then be free for meditating on
the "mysteries of light".

This indication is not intended to limit a
rightful freedom in personal and community
prayer, where account needs to be taken of spiritual and pastoral needs and of the occurrence of
particular liturgical celebrations which might
call for suitable adaptations. What is really important is that the Rosary should always be seen
and experienced as a path of contemplation. In
the Rosary, in a way similar to what takes place
in the Liturgy, the Christian week, centred on
Sunday, the day of Resurrection, becomes a
journey through the mysteries of the life of
Christ, and he is revealed in the lives of his disciples as the Lord of time and of history.

(*RVM*, 29-38)

www.ingramcontent.com/pod-product-compliance
Lightning Source LLC
Chambersburg PA
CBHW072345090426
42741CB00012B/2933